NGOs and Rural Development

About the Author

Joel S.G.R. Bhose has 22 years of long and rich experience of working with NGos in rural development. He earned his Bachelor's Degree in Economics, Master Degree in Social Work and Post-Graduate Diploma in Personnel Management. While doing his M. Phil. Futurology, he conducted a study on 40 NGOs working in the field of rural development. He has also completed a course in Development Management. He has held various positions at St. Andrew's Project and in CASA.

Presently Mr. Bose is working as Head, Department of Training and Development at Meenakshi Mission Hospital and Research Centre, Madurai. Also, he is Adviser to Mahesemam Women's Project, Consultant to CONSORT and Chief Editor of CONSORT News Bulletin. He is a visiting faculty as well at Madurai Kamraj University.

NGOs AND RURAL DEVELOPMENT
Theory and Practice

JOEL S.G.R. BHOSE
M.A. (S.W.), D.P.H., M.Phil (fu), D.M.

CONCEPT PUBLISHING COMPANY, NEW DELHI-110059

ISBN 81-7022-732-1

First Published 2003

Published and Printed by
Ashok Kumar Mittal
Concept Publishing Company
A/15-16, Commercial Block, Mohan Garden,
NEW DELHI-110059 (India)

Phone : 5351460, 5351794
Fax : 091-11-5357103
Cable : CONPUBCO
Email : publishing@conceptpub.com

FOREWORD

Mr. Joel S.G.R. Bhose, who is Consultant for Consortium of Service Organisations in Tamilnadu (CONSORT), is a hard worker, sincere, intelligent, confident and courageous, a character of surprising force, capacity, shrewdness and determination. Now, I realize the other part of Mr. Joel as a good academician and patriotic yearning for the Rural Development. He has taken stupendous effort for this valuable inscription.

Being the President of Consortium of Service Organisations in Tamilnadu (CONSORT) I strongly believe that once the community is truly organized, then the job in developing the community is half done. The communities could be organized only by the NGOs who involve themselves in social development. As the author clearly depicts, the Rural development and voluntary action is not a 9 to 5 job, it is a long process which involves commitment, involvement and sacrifice of the social worker/NGO.

It is my view that NGOs are part of the Government who blessed with;

a chance to be the agent of change for the betterment of the needy

a chance to organize a new society where all of us may live in peace and harmony.

The functional effectiveness of the NGOs involved in Community development is mainly depends on consistent availability of funds. However, lack of reliable information and importance of the community also hamper the effective functioning of them. This book gives clear information for the sustainable development of the NGOs who yearn for knowledge.

In the first four chapters the book focuses on the Evolution of NGOs in rural development and categories of voluntarism. In the fifth and sixth chapter the author dealt with concept of rural development and NGOs interventions in rural development. In the remaining chapters, he provides detailed and valuable information on people's participation in rural development, importance of empowering the rural people and emphasizes the need for advocacying to influence the government to make policy changes in favour of the poor.

I am sure that this book would not only bridge up the information gap between the NGOs and Rural Development, but also serve as a source book, providing guidelines, knowledge, information regarding rural development to the researchers, academics, students, government officials, agencies and other stakeholders who are really interested and involved themselves in developing rural India.

I whole heartedly congratulate the author and the publisher for their relenetless effort in bringing out this master piece. I wish them all success.

Dr. N. Sethuraman
Founder President
Consortium of Service Organisations
in Tamil Nadu (CONSORT)

PREFACE

This book entitled "NGOs in Rural And Development — Theory and Practice" is the outcome of the effort in theoritising my long and rich experience with reputed NGOs like CASA etc., research studies and learnings from variety of NGOs working at Micro and Macro level.

I would forcibly state that "People's Development is People's Business, If so, a question may arise as to what roles need NGOs to play to all?

NGOs are supposed to facilitate the people to carry out their journey of development.

In the facilitating process, NGOs have multiple roles like organising, educating, motivating, guiding, awareness creating, training, capacity building, empowering, advocacying, lobbying etc. to bring about desired rural development. They can never substitute Peoples roles.

As a person working with the NGO Sector, for the past 22 years, I feel that NGOs who are supposed to empower the people need to get professionally empowered, philosophically enriched and conceptually enlightened. NGOs are, no doubt, deeply committed in their field work. But they need to improve the conceptual clarities and managerial and professional capacities.

There has always been an inspiration within me to speak about the good works of NGOs, to write about their specialities, and reflect upon their interventions critically for the benefit of the NGOs themselves and NGO related agencies, be it donors, Government authorities, bankers and other stakeholders in Rural Development and faculty members and students of NGO Management, Rural Development, Social Work, Sociology, Rural Management etc. Keeping in view of the aforesaid audience particularly the persons working with NGOs, this book is constituted with 10 chapters which would give all basic inputs related to theories and practices of NGOs.

Chapter 1 highlights why at all there is a need for NGOs in Rural Development. Chapter 2 describes the evolution and growth of voluntary organisations. In chapter 3, I have evolved a theory of voluntarisms such as 1. Sacrificial Voluntarism 2. Professional and Developmental voluntarism, 3. Amateur Xerox copy voluntarism. 4. Ventilatory voluntarism, 5. Survival voluntarism. 6. Pseudo voluntarism. Chapter 4 defines that "Voluntary organisations are Non-Profit making agencies that are constituted with a vision by a group of like minded people, committed for the uplift of the poor, marginalised, unprivileged, underprivileged, impoverished, downtrodden and the needy and they are closer and accessible to the target groups, flexible in administration, quicker in decision-making, timely in action and facilitating the people towards self-reliance ensuring their fullest participation in the whole process of development."

Chapter 5 throws light on the concept of Development, Rural Development and Voluntary Action. "Development is not a product but it is a process. It is not NGOs itinerary but People's Agenda. It is not entisting donors but conscientising people. It is not a 9 a.m. to 5 p.m. job but it is a long process that requires commitment, conviction and sacrifice on the part of the community workers. NGOs need to take up hard tasks like attitudinal and behaviour changes. Peoples management is NGOs' destination and at that point they must come out from the communities allowing them to function of their own to exercise control over their living environment.

Chapter 6 portrays the specialities of NGOs as what the Government could not do and what corporate Sector did not do have been achieved by Voluntary Organisations. The moment one thinks of Voluntary Organisations, it comes to mind that they are *'pro-people'* Some say that NGOs are behind the people catalysing the development process. Some others say that the people are behind the NGOs and only on People's Strength the NGOs proceed the journey of development. In fact, they are both within themselves as partners of development. The relationship between them is humanitarian, professional and philosophical as the situation demands. In chapter 7, it is observed that "Development without People's Participation is like that of a wheel without spokes. Participation presupposes belongingness and culminates in control and ownership. Hence, development sans people's participation means development sans development". Chapter 8 highlights the importance of advocacy function of NGOs "Advocacy means influencing Policy in favour of the poor and powerless. This otherwise, means a misfavour to the power holders." However much, NGOs carry out service delivery and socio-economic development programmes with commitment, development of the poor and the powerless becomes partial, incomplete, transitory and fleeting unless policies are made in favour of them.

Chapter 9 highlights the crying need for NGOs to perform empowering role. NGOs need to understand that "while charity means giving something to people, empowerment shall mean giving power and authority to people". Obviously, empowerment is about power, and about changing the balance of power, The term 'empowerment' refers to a range of activities from individual self-assertion to collective resistance, protest and mobilisation that challenge basic power relations. Empowerment, therefore is a process aimed at changing the nature and direction of systemic forces which marginalize Dalits, Tribes, Women and other disadvantaged sections in a given context.

In the concluding 10th Chapter a swot analysis on NGO has been made. NGOs must clearly understand that people predominantly require motivation than money, awareness than materials, information than inputs supply education than doles, empathy than sympathy, guidance than gifts, facilitation than contribution, opportunities than charities. NGOs must first become thinking organisations.

NGOs' thrust must be on building people. NGOs by and large, must improve their professional knowledge, skill and competence to meet the needs of the day. There is a crying need for NGOs to seriously look into the impact of "Zations"(i.e.) globalisation, modernizations, standardization, liberalization, industrialization, commercialization etc. NGOs need to think globally and act locally. NGOs are supposed to be only catalysts who could operate objectively, empathetically and professionally. Development work is no longer a favour to the poor. It is people's legitimate right and NGOs have to rightly understand it, Net working of people's Organisations is the key and most significant function of today's NGOs. The true success of NGO is not the receipt of national awards or getting international rewards but only the victory or glory to the people over their poverty and injustices.

It does not matter whether it is a small NGO, or a big NGO or a large NGO or a mighty NGO or an old NGO or a young NGO. What matters is whether one is a professional NGO with a Profound commitment and perserving will. **By professional NGO, I refer to 'the' voluntary organisation to which people are its heart,**

commitment is its spinal card, professionalism is its brain and values are its lungs. Strong in one aspect and weak in the other may not serve the purpose totally and completely. Hence a full fledged NGO must be committed, People centred, Professional, honest and value based and I am hopeful that this book will serve as a tool to fulfil such criteria among voluntary organisation and to bring about desired rural development.

JOEL S. G. R. BHOSE

CONTENTS

1

Why At All NGOs In Rural Development

Service is the Rent we pay for the
privilege of living on the Earth

— *Eldon Tanner*

This Chapter explains in brief the need and importance of Non-Governmental Organisations (NGOs) in Rural Development. The current rural problems, the threats of macro forces upon rural communities and the challenges before NGOs have also been analysed.

We all agree that there is no substitute for hardwork. We must also agree that there is no comparison at all for the voluntary work of NGOs.

Non-Governmental Organisations (NGOs) are rendering their services with a voluntary spirit for the uplift of millions of rural people in the country.

They involve in the development of the rural poor with a profound commitment and a strong will. As their minds are geared up with voluntarism or altruism they do not mind their personal sufferings, discomforts, inconveniences and stresses in the process of their intervention. It is true and not an exaggeration that NGOs' pains and strains turn out to be a pleasure for them when the poor people gain something concretely.

NGOs are the ones who really intend to care the uncared sections and the people at the bottom of the social stratum. Their work is people centred and hence they reach the unreached rural poor and live and work with them. They strive to promote the lives of the oppressed, deprived, marginalised, impoverished, downtrodden, hopelost, helpless, powerless, deserted and poverty stricken in the rural areas. The justification as to why NGOs are to exist is that such ignored subjects of the country are truely the primary subject matter for them. They carryout their work with a humanitarian concern coupled with professional wisdom for the betterment and sustainable development of the poor communities with the involvement of the people themselves.

People's development requires rather necessitates voluntarism, commitment, devotion, dedication and sometimes sacrifices too. NGOs are bestowed with the aforesaid characteristics and the personnel and the development workers are endowed with a spirit of voluntarism and concern for the impoverished. It is generally believed that NGOs have close access to the people and their efforts are very much benefiting rural communities. They have a definite 'Say' and 'Identity' with the people for their committed approach and timely action and hence they have gained a "Solmen Command" and "Bastion of Support" of the people with whom they work. NGOs are known for their pristine spirit and creative dynamism. Their services are undoubtedly commendable in the uplift of the rural poor. That is why NGOs' works are quoted as 'Noble and Yeoman Services'.

Let us now proceed to analyse the magnitude of rural problems and threats. Followed by that, status and the interventions of NGOs and the current challenges before them are also examined.

1. RURAL PROBLEMS

In India more than 70 per cent of the population dwell in villages. There are about 6 lakhs villages constituting more than 600 million people. The problems of rural masses are terrible and innumerable. Even after 50 years of independence, people in villages are found to be economically backward, socially oppressed, culturally suppressed, politically exploited, traditionally nullified and in general deprived of facilities like health, education, transportation, communication and even denied basic amenities like protected drinking water, food, clothing, shelter etc. As a result they are prone to poverty, illiteracy, ignorance, ill health and multitudes of exploitations. They resort to attribute their plight to fate and destiny blaming themselves without analysing critically the causative factors for their backwardness, poverty and injustice.

1.1 Poverty

"Poverty is the major problem still in the Rural India". Statistics reveal that the percentage of people below poverty line goes on a downward trend, but not the aggregate number of people. According to the Expert Group (1993) the poverty ratio in rural area has come down from 33.4 per cent during 1987-88 to 28.4 per cent in 1993-94 but the actual number of people below poverty line has raisen from 229.4 million to 244 million during the same period. In other words India is the country wherein the largest number of poor people are being accommodated. (However the Government of India estimates that the number of people living below poverty line are only 141 million during 1993-94).

Table 1.1 : Population below the Poverty Line

(i) As per the Planning Commission, GOI

S. No.	Sector	1983-84	1984-85	1987-88	1989-90	1993-94
				Population in Millions		
1.	Rural	221.5	222.2	196.0	168.6	141.1
2.	Urban	49.5	50.5	41.7	42.2	27.1
3.	Total	271.0	272.7	237.7	210.8	168.2
				Poverty Ratio (%)		
4.	Rural	40.4	39.9	33.4	28.4	21.7
5.	Urban	28.1	27.7	20.1	19.3	11.6
6.	Total	37.4	36.9	29.9	25.3	18.9

(ii) As per the Expert Group (1993)

S. No.	Sector	1983-84	1987-88	1993-94
		Population in Millions		
1.	Rural	251.7	229.4	244.0
2.	Urban	75.3	83.4	76.3
3.	Total	327.0	312.8	320.3
		Poverty Ratio (%)		
4.	Rural	39.9	33.4	28.4
5.	Urban	27.7	20.1	19.3
6.	Total	36.9	29.9	25.3

Source : (i) CMIE, India's Social Sectors, Feb. 1996.
(ii) CSO, Press Report.

Table 1.2 : Incidence of Rural and Urban Poverty - State wise

S. No.	State/UT	Rural 1973-74	1977-78	1983	1987-88	1993-94	Urban 1973-74	1977-78	1983	1987-88	1993-94
(1)	(2)	(3)	(4)	(5)	(6)	(7)	(8)	(9)	(10)	(11)	(12)
1.	Andhra Pradesh	48.4	38.1	26.5	20.9	15.92	52.6	46.5	40.1	44.6	38.33
2.	Arunachal Pradesh	52.7	59.8	42.6	39.4	45.01	37.2	37.6	26.4	17.3	7.73
3.	Assam	52.7	59.8	42.6	39.4	45.01	37.2	37.6	26.4	17.3	7.73
4.	Bihar	63.0	63.3	64.4	52.6	58.21	51.8	52.2	50.4	57.7	34.50
5.	Goa	46.9	37.6	14.8	17.6	5.34	36.9	36.7	27.2	33.7	27.03
6.	Gujarat	46.4	41.8	29.8	28.7	22.18	49.3	43.1	40.6	39.6	27.89
7.	Hariyana	34.2	27.7	20.6	16.2	28.02	39.6	36.2	23.5	17.8	16.38
8.	Himachal Pradesh	27.4	33.5	17.0	16.3	30.34	13.2	19.5	9.3	6.2	9.18
9.	Jammu & Kashmir	45.5	42.9	26.0	25.7	30.34	30.4	31.9	17.1	14.8	9.18
10.	Karnataka	55.1	48.2	36.3	32.8	29.88	52.0	52.9	43.4	49.1	40.14
11.	Kerala	59.2	51.5	39.0	29.1	25.76	62.2	59.5	48.7	43.4	24.55
12.	Madhya Pradesh	62.7	62.5	48.9	41.9	40.64	58.3	62.1	54.6	48.2	48.38
13.	Maharashtra	57.7	64.0	45.2	40.8	37.93	43.0	40.6	40.6	39.0	35.15
14.	Manipur	52.7	59.8	42.6	39.4	45.01	37.2	37.6	26.4	17.3	7.73
15.	Meghalaya	52.7	59.8	42.6	39.4	45.01	37.2	37.6	26.4	17.3	7.73
16.	Mizoram	52.7	59.8	42.6	39.4	45.01	37.2	37.6	26.4	17.3	7.73
17.	Nagaland	52.7	59.8	42.6	39.4	45.01	37.2	37.6	26.4	17.3	7.73
18.	Orissa	67.3	72.4	67.53	57.6	49.72	56.3	53.6	50.63	44.1	41.64
19.	Punjab	28.2	16.4	13.2	12.6	11.95	27.7	27.6	23.9	12.9	11.35
20.	Rajasthan	44.8	35.9	33.5	33.2	26.46	53.2	46.4	40.4	39.0	30.49
21.	Sikkim	52.7	59.8	42.6	39.4	45.01	37.2	37.6	26.4	17.3	7.73
22.	Tamil Nadu	57.4	57.7	54.0	45.8	32.48	54.5	53.2	49.2	43.9	39.77
23.	Tripura	52.7	59.8	42.6	39.4	45.01	37.2	37.6	26.4	17.3	7.73

Table-1.2 (Contd.)

(1)	(2)	(3)	(4)	(5)	(6)	(7)	(8)	(9)	(10)	(11)	(12)
24.	Uttar Pradesh	56.4	47.6	46.5	41.1	42.28	59.5	57.1	50.3	45.2	35.39
25.	West Bengal	73.2	68.3	63.1	48.3	40.80	34.5	38.7	32.2	32.8	22.41
	UTs										
26.	Delhi	24.4	30.2	7.7	1.3	1.90	49.2	33.3	28.3	16.9	16.03
27.	A & N Islands	57.4	57.75	54.0	45.8	32.48	54.5	53.2	49.2	43.9	39.77
28.	Chandigarh	27.7	27.6	23.9	12.9	11.35	27.7	27.6	23.9	12.9	11.35
29.	Daman & Diu	46.9	37.6	14.8	17.6	5.34	36.9	36.7	27.20	33.7	27.03
30.	Lakshadweep	59.2	51.5	39.0	29.1	25.76	62.2	59.5	48.7	43.4	24.55
31.	Pondicherry	57.4	57.7	54.0	45.8	32.48	54.5	53.2	49.2	43.9	39.77
	All India	56.4	53.1	45.6	39.1	37.27	49.2	47.4	42.2	40.01	32.46

Source : 1. Report of the Expert Group on Estimation of Proportion and Number of Poor, Planning Commission, July, 1993.
2. Press Note from CSO.

In statewise observation as per the report of the expert group in July 93, it is found that the rural poverty ratio during 93-94 stands at 58.21 per cent in Bihar the highest, 49.72 per cent in Orissa and 45.01 per cent in Arunachal Pradesh, Assam, Manipur, Megalaya, Mizoram, Nagaland and Thripura. The chronic poverty is primarily attributed to proliferating population despite varied family planning measures. Rural poor particularly landless labour families tend to feel comfortable that 'more children means more wages'. Hence in a sense poverty attributes to rising population and vice versa.

There is a critical view that population is not the real problem in India but the improper distribution of resources and opportunities. It is a paradox that such a naturally resourced country carries so many poverty - striken deprived and poor people. It is a sad truth that 80 per cent of the National Wealth has been cornered and garnered by 20 per cent elites - among them too largest to a very few, larger to few and rest to the other few and simply the 20 per cent of the left outs are left-out to the 80 per cent left outs.

1.2 Casteism

Casteism is deep rooted in the Indian Society and particularly in rural areas. The evils of casteism nullify *Daliths* and keep them under suppression. Constitutional guarantee and legal rights go futile among the traditional caste blended rural societies. In a sense socio cultural bondages leave the *daliths* and tribes under disguised/infinite slavery.

1.3 Women's Exploitation

Women's exploitation is very much found in villages. The most suppressed are the women of the oppressed classes. Numerous social controls and rules are imposed on women under cultural pretext which block the women folk from emerging towards lime light. Of course, it is a milestone in the history of India that the 73rd amendment ensures one third reservation for women. But it is misfortunate that their husbands perform their roles as play back singers.

1.4 Rural Unemployment

Rural unemployment remains a herculean problem in the nation. Rural employment opportunities largely depend upon agriculture and allied activities as Indian economy still remains an agriculture economy.

1.5. Unremunerative Agriculture

Agriculture, the primary occupation of millions is unremunerative. Agriculture is deemed as a gambling of monsoon. When North India is flooded, South dries. Even within a State when one part is over poured the other part is drought hit. For instance in States like A.P., the Krishna and Godavari regions are marooned while Telengana and Rayalaseema regions long for rain drops. The Cauvery Delta of Trichy and Tanjore Districts of Tamil Nadu that were well blessed with the bountiful irrigation are also now left at the mercy of Karnataka. Earlier irrigation to the farmers was only attributed to nature but it has become a political issue affecting both the States. Like this there are many other similar cases in the country.

There is an old saying that Indian peasant is born in debt lives in debt, dies in debt and bequeaths debt to his generation. Credit needs of the farmers could not be met by the nationalised Banks duly and timely. There were umpteen suicidal cases among farming communities in the various parts of the country particularly the cotton cultivators in A.P. in the year 1999 owing to unshoulderable loan burdens.

Agriculture labourers ever remain labourers for generations and they never become owners except in a few cases. Too many till in too little lands.

1.6. Lack of Basic Amenities

Rural people are deprived of basic amenities and infrastructures. Even after 5 decades of Independence many villages are not provided with protected drinking water. Massive calamities like Latur earthquake and the super cyclone at Orissa, the terrific earthquake in Gujarat caused irrepairable damages that worst affected the rural areas. It may take a decade and more to restore normalcy economically and Socially. Sanitation is poor. It is a sad plight that people particularly women in the rural areas have to avail road-sides during nights to attend to natural calls. This may be due to lack of awareness as well as lack of infrastructural facilities. Literacy is still low (particularly female literacy). Infrastructures like roads, communication, marketing facilities, credit facilities etc. are also denied to many remote villages in the country.

Though leaders like Mahatma Gandhi clarioned that "India lives in villages and villages are the backbone of our country" our politicians and bureaucrats could not achieve a desired rural development. The marvellous 5 years plan and programmes like Green Revolution did not yield fruitful benefits for the poor as the same were not designed as people centred. On the other hand the growth of a few mighty industries resulted in mass production by machinery quelling the opportunities of production by the masses.

1.7. Denial of Information

Another important lacuna is that the rural communities are denied information. The Future Society as Allwyn Tofflar says would be an information society. India itself lags behind in the information systems and technologies and rural society is very much lacking in this. Information is knowledge. Knowledge is power. Indian rural society appears to be powerless not only because of economic poverty but also due to information poverty. Only now States like A.P. make a beginning to focus on information technology.

1.8. Government Policies

Governmental policies and programmes are not very much favourable to the rural poor as they are still treated as passive recipients and humble beneficiaries even after the formulation of **SJSY (Swarna Jayanthi Swarozgar Yojana).** The rural communities are by and large ignored by politicians and bureacrats. As they are unorganised they are vulnerable to oppression and susceptible to suppression. In certain cases rural poor are being tantalised.

The Government's budget allocation to the rural poor is also low in terms of their needs. The rural society is prone to multitudes of exploitation on the one side by one set of people and silent negligence on the other side by the various responsible intervening authorities at various levels. The emotions and voices of the poor are being gratified by the political Government in terms of petty charities, feeble doles, tiny subsidies and mean gifts like sarees and dhoties. Governments are run more on political than social objectives. Also Government is a huge and large machinery governed by hard and fast rules. Despite ample resources like personnel, infrastructure and funds, the Government programmes do not reach the villages timely, justly and fully due to in-built bureaucracy and other inherrant limitations in that system. India no doubt progresses but slowly and feebly. While there are some forces to uplift the rural poor, there are many threats to hamper their growth.

1.9. Political Instability

Political instability remains a great threat to the fragile rural economy. Between 1996 and 99, India faced three parliament elections as Governments fell down on account of political wrestlings. Hung parliaments could not execute concrete programmes for the uplift of the rural poor.

2. TREATS OF "ZATIONS"

It is sad to understand that many NGOs in the country are either unaware or unmindful of the current macro interventions.

By **ZATIONS** I refer to what is popularly used such as Globali**zation**, Standardi**zation**, Liberali**zation**, Moderni**zation**, etc., that are nurtured and propagated by the **World Trade Organization** as a consequence of which poor are being pushed down, as many believe, towards Marginali**zation.**

Hence NGOs of all types and at all levels need to be conscious, aware and sensitive about the global scenario and the market economy and protect the interests of the poor and downtrodden. This is the real challenge before the NGOs of the 21st century. Hence brief observations and critical analyses have been presented here to benefit the NGO persons to be prepared to respond to and deal with issues and problems at the micro level vis-a-vis macro issues.

2.1 Loss of Control of Farmers

The national consultation group met at Institute of Social and Economic Change (ISEC) Bangalore observes that "at no time has there been such a loss of control from individual peasants in what they should plant. the price at which they can sell what they grow; and also in the very resources that are fundamental in their definition of their identity and their self. For instance, in the formulation of the intellectual property rights regime of WTO. This leads to the loot of the genetic resource. There is, at this moment, more than 400 prospectors of trans-national medical corporations in our country are establishing direct relationship with the tribes. They are prospecting for genetic resources that they can take back, isolate the medicines in their labs, and then market them. There is a fear of loss of control of the nation itself".

2.2 Deteriorating Ecosystems

The remarkably diverse ecosystems, the natural resources which are the source of livelihood for many are under threat. This is because the economic policy needs export. One could argue it is needed because of national debt, but this debt is because of import of goods needed for the elite. Only 5 per cent of our population have cars. The import of a large number of goods have put pressure on our foreign exchange. This movement from development to export led growth has implications on the sustainability of the rural economy.

The aqua culture federation of India claims that the world is looking to India for its shrimp needs, and seeks to increase export from 70,000 tonnes to 2,00,000 tonnes. This is despite knowing the enormous amounts of ecological disaster.

Coastal area eco-systems are in peril. Market forces attracted farmers and facilitated proliferation of prawn farms. Hundreds of thousands of acres of paddy fields and agricultural lands were converted into prawn farms. Of course, prawn farmers celebrated their hay day during 90s for a year or two. But the prawn culture suffered a miserable set back due to virus attack on the dollar fetching prawns. Year after year farmers invested with high hopes on prawn tanks but reaped nothing. They could not repay the loan. Due to mounting debt-pressure they had to sell their lands at the rock-bottom price to the fittest survivors, the big farmers.

In certain cases prawn farmers tried to reconvert their lands for agricultural purposes. But their efforts were not fruitful because underneath the earth the water zone had been turned into saline zone as a consequence of which villagers could not get even drinking water. Another tragedy is that the cattle wealth dwindled and subsidiary occupations like dairy, goat-rearing, sheep-rearing etc., in prawn prone villages disappeared. Farmers who were running milk co-operative societies and supplying milk to the nearby towns now depend upon outsiders for their own domestic consumptions. Around aqua farms thousands of palm trees and lakhs of coconut trees are withering away.

In a study conducted by the author himself on behalf of CASA in 1999 on the socio-economic conditions of coastal villages in Krishna, Guntur, East Godavari and West Godavari Districts it was observed that the farmers have lost many of their livelihood like cultivation of paddy, vegetable gardening, agricultural labour, catching fish in the local ponds and canals, rearing milch cattle, goat, sheep, duck etc. Some farmers shared their sad truth that the yield of coconuts has come down to 30 per cent in 1999 when compared with 1992 and 80 per cent of the coconut trees would be withering away in a decade if the same trend continues. Many farmers realised that their daily living is difficult as their options of livelihood disappeared on account of advent of massive prawn culture.

Aqua culture has also brought wide spread destruction of mangrove forests, affecting coastal environment.

Deforestation for commercial causes are devastating the core of the eco-system.

Mining is another area where laws are being modified to accommodate export needs and other trans-nationals, notably Australian. The Australians propose to prospect 50,000 acres. What will be the implications on the ecosystems, on the people, is anybody's guess.

In agriculture, vast changes can be seen in the crops grown and in cropping patterns. There is monoculturization. As a result of this, 7 varieties of rice are grown in 70 per cent of our area, from tens of thousands before the green revolution. Pepsi wants only one variety of tomato for its ketchup. Kentucky Fried Chicken wants only an imported variety of Chicken, fed on an imported variety of maize. All these varieties lead to monocultures, loss of biodiversity, and leave the farmer at the mercy of the trans-nationals.

Millions of acres of lands are being purchased by companies to promote modernised farms and industries. The poor farmers who found their lands uproductive due to lack of infra structure facilities disposed their lands at a throw-away price to such enterprises and become labourers in the farms or factories promoted by elite entrepreneurs. In a sense, the owner of a small land holding is being marginalised to a daily wage-earner.

2.3 Reversal of Land Ceiling Act

There is tremendous pressure to reverse land ceiling acts from many sections of society-politicians, big industrial houses, editors and big farmers. The argument is that small holdings are not conducive for India to become self-sufficient in food. There has been pressure on the former Minister for Environment and Forest Kamal Nath, to denotify and give 'degraded' forests to the industry. Though the merits could be debated, the denotification of protected forests for industrial use is a threat to the well being of the ecosystem.

2.4 Polarization of Wealth

In the last 30 years, the gap between the top 20 per cent of the population and the bottom 20 per cent has doubled. Those at the bottom are losing control over their natural resources. This is a global phenomenon. The top 358 billionaires have income and wealth more than 2.5 billion dollars.

Large scale displacement, feminization of poverty, increased rural-urban migration, widespread destruction of livelihood systems of the poor etc. have increased with alarming speed.

Market economy is concerned more with profit than people. The commercial interest will not be conducive to the common populace.

If globalization is pivoted around business rather than human consideration that may jeopardise the livelihood of the poor masses in countries like India.

2.5 WTO Vs. Labour and Environmental Standards

To simply put, the WTO is a Worldwide Organisation formed in 1995 which makes trade between countries possible. Before the WTO came into existence, trade was conducted under General Agreement on Tariffs and Trade. Because of the WTO, which has 135 countries as members, the whole world can now be considered as one market.

People believe that poorer countries are getting destroyed due to this free trade between countries. There are some organisations which believe that when countries organise trade, the needs of the local people are overlooked. They say though it is called free trade, it is not free at all but the rich countries benefit at the cost of the poor. As S. Gurumurthy comments that "according to rich countries the goods made by the developing nations in breach of what the west regards as the standards for labour and environment should be banned for import in the west". It means that from the crackers made in Sivakasi in Tamil Nadu to the carpets made in Rajasthan and UP, to the beedi made in Kerala and Karnataka, a vast array of items would be banned for import in the west just because they employ labour, including child labour, without the minimum standards of labour applicable in the west. Likewise, goods made in violation of the environment standards of the west too would be banned. The MNCs are unable to face the competition from the cheap goods manufactured by the cheap labour in India, which is one of our competitive advantages.

Earlier, if the Indian Government felt that TVs made in Japan are not good for the country it could increase the customs duty to make them more expensive than the ones produced in India. Now, under WTO rules, this would be wrong. The result is that many foreign-made TVs are available cheaply, whereas many Indian brands have disappeared. The positive thing is it is possible to sell Indian Milk in Denmark, U.K. or the US. But this is not happening because producing milk in these countries is cheaper than producing it here. This is because the cattle feed which costs Rs. 100/- is given to the farmers down upto Rs. 5 in these countries. India being a poor country cannot sell the cattle feed cheaply to farmers. Also productivity of the cattle is remarkably higher there than here.

So, though it is called free trade India loses out in the long run. Under WTO rules India can approach the Dispute Settlement Body which will decide who has broken the rules.

The World Trade for most people means to buy or sell things. But for WTO it means anything where money is involved. It includes goods, services and intellectual property.

Under patent provision, two Japanese men applied for a patent on curry. They called the curry, that is cooked in most Indian homes, their invention! Under WTO rules these two men would get royalties on all export or import of curry or curry product in Japan.

This is covered under intellectual property rights. Some people have tried to patent even Basmati rice, extracts and turmeric goods, which are grown/produced and sold by millions of farmers.

One of the most basic aims of WTO is to bring down barriers of Trade between countries. But US wants a ban on products made with the use of child labour. The four rich countries i.e. the US, Canada, Japan and the European Union want a clause to keep out products from countries where products are manufactured without taking into consideration the harm to environment.

India is against these clauses as these would be used to stop products like carpets, handlooms and other products which are produced in rural and cottage industries.

(Words to know in the Context of Globalization)

WTO : The World Trade Organisation is the only international agency overseeing the rules of international trade. Its purpose is to help trade flow smoothly.

MNCs : Multi National Companies

TRIPS : Agreement on Trade Related Aspects of Intellectual Property. This deals with such issues as copyright, trademarks, patents, industrial designs and trade secrets.

TRIMS : Trade Related Investment Measures.

MFN : Most-Favoured Nation. This means that each member country has to treat all its fellow members equally - it cannot discriminate between members. If one country grants another country a special favour (such as a lower duty rate) that favour also has to be given to other WTO members so that they are all equally "most-favoured".

GATT : General Agreement on Tariffs and Trade.

GATS : General Agreement on Trade in Services.

Copy Right : The rights of authors of literary artistic works are protected by copyright. This also includes a number of creative efforts like musical instruments, paintings, computer programmes etc.

TARIFFS : The taxes Countries impose on goods being imported or exported.

PATENT : The protection given to inventions, industrial property, Trademarks, designs.

SUBSIDY : The support price given by the Government.

3. STATUS OF NGOs

Currently the NGOs have emerged as a third sector in the country and the rest of the world, next to the Government and the corporate sector.

The late 1970s saw people coming out of the church, the left, the Gandhian and Lohiaites movements to converge in the field of development at the grassroots with focus on awareness creation and conscientization.

Pragmatism, combined with the need to improve the life situation of the poor, soon made people from all streams to talk of development by mid 1980s. The fragmented, compartmentalized development work which still had charity and service orientation soon was replaced by integrated development models by the late 1980s. The structural obstacles placed at each level of activity and the need to influence the policies gave rise to the "empowerment models" by early 1990s. Gender justice, environmental concerns, human rights (more appropriately, in a country like India, the basic socio-economic-cultural rights) etc. were understood to be part and parcel of the structural aspects of the society which, apart from class, caste and ethnicity, also were responsible for the exploitation of the marginalized sections of the society.

The external donors' pro-active role and global events provided a macro perspective to the grassroots work with the perspective of structural alleviation of poverty and exploitation through sustainable development processes by integrating gender, environment and human right concerns into the process. Together with development, the NGOs developed the perspective of participatory processes (as against the top-down and centralized approach of the political and governance system) and many started practising them at the grassroots to strengthen self-management and grassroot democracy. Thus from the charity-service and different ideologies of early 1970s emerged the concept of sustainable development in mid 1990s with quite a number of NGOs following this perspective. This however, does not mean that all the NGOs belong to the same category. Over the wide spectrum of NGOs in India one could find various types of NGOs.

During 1990s the number of NGOs in India have multiplied many fold. An estimated over 30,000 NGOs, most of them with rural focus, are actively working. NGOs have acquired legitimacy and credibility to a great extent, notwithstanding charges of corruption and lack of public accountability and transparency on some NGOs.

NGOs find a place in many government and semi-government policy and implementation bodies. With the failure of the state in reaching the poor and the marginalized NGOs in India have come to play a very important role. As a part of civil society the NGOs' role in micro-macro linkages and policy advocacy has become a dominant feature now.

To keep in line with the process of privatization, the state has gradually been following the principle of social contracting with the NGOs in implementing its anti-poverty programme, thus providing lot of space for the NGOs to collaborate with the governments in power. At the same time, the NGOs together with the marginalized sections of the society are actively involved in opposing the policies of the State and Governments which are detrimental to the livelihood systems of the poor.

The structural adjustment, liberalization and privatization practices pursued under the New Economic Policy during the past half decade, while linking India to the process of globalization under market forces have simultaneously destroyed the livelihood systems of the poor as, for example, in the case of the coastal belt. While India's foreign exchange/ balance of payment position seems to be much better, the fact remains that its poor and marginalized have been further marginalized.

While within the political party spectrum there has been opposition from some corners, by and large there is a consensus on the economic policies pursued. The difference is only on the speed and checks and balances! In such a situation it is the NGOs, particularly those who are actively involved in micro-macro linkages and policy advocacy oppose the wrong policies.

As NGOs are well versed in community motivation and social mobilization they are being increasingly involved in all rural projects and programmes by the Government, be it locally sponsored or funded by international agencies. The current five year plans too lay greater emphasis on NGOs' involvement in all the development programmes for the rural poor. It is for the NGOs to decide whether to offer total collaboration or critical collaboration after analysing the level and intensity of the pro-poor components in the said programmes. (Further details can be referred to in Chapter - 2 and 4).

4. THE CHALLENGE BEFORE NGOs

NGOs' works related to current context and the ensuing challenges pertinent to emerging global scenario are being briefed here.

Now the role of NGOs is very much a challenging one. In the current scenario of the 21st Century, as observed by Anita Cheria and Edwin, the NGOs face the dual task of collaborating critically with the State and at the same time fighting against the anti-people/anti-marginalized policy. Such a dual task cannot be discharged effectively unless the NGOs have autonomy based on the self-reliant capabilities. NGOs' sustained intervention will depend very much in future on their self-reliant capacity and local resource mobilization.

The paradigm of mainstream development indicates that such model is not sustainable in the ultimate analysis. Its anti-people, anti-women, anti-environment, anti-sustainable thrust have done irreversible damage and destruction. Yet, the process of globalization is pursued with alarming speed. While opposing this destructive approach, one cannot wait to see the reversal of this policy in the given global context. What is urgently needed is to develop and strengthen micro-level people centered and self-managed models. Grass-root level micro-banking systems, community resource management, collective and cooperative income generation activities etc. are possible models.

Globalization is inevitable and standardization, as many believe, is a necessary evil. The NGOs of the 21st Century need to function as sensitive, critical and intellectual organizations to protect the interest of the poor and downtrodden.

With the 73rd constitutional amendment on Panchayat Raj Institution [PRI], new opportunities and challenges are opened up at the grassroots for the NGOs. Since the village level Panchayat elections are supposed to be fought without any political party symbol (supposed to be a non-party event!) it provides a very good opportunity for the NGOs to educate and enable the poor to enter into the local level governance. The PRIs, with their proximity of the people, are within the reach of the people whereas higher level bodies are not.

One-third reservation for women and one-third reservation for the socially oppressed and economically exploited dalits makes it possible to change the content of these local governance bodies. With proper education, training and strategies, it is possible for the enlightened and capable poor women and men to not only enter into these bodies democratically but also give new dynamism to the bottom-up development process. Strengthening of these grassroot democratic bodies will have a cumulative effect on the polity of the country.

While some NGOs have focused on this aspect of grassroot process, a large numbers haven't realized the potential. The NGOs over the years have promoted vast social infrastructure of the poor, the women, the dalits etc. Enabling them to influence the policies and to enter into governance at least in the grassroots, and strengthening local level democracy will go a long way to improve the life situation of the poor and empower them further. This will sustain the initiative of the people for sustained growth and development.

The sustainability of the grassroot level people centered participatory and self-managed development processes will ultimately depend on the capability of the people in local resource mobilization and influencing policy processes. Mere assertion of rights through social mobilization and democratic pressure will not satisfy their basic and development needs.

Enhancing the governance at the local level and bringing in a qualitative change in the local bodies in favour of the poor and marginalized could integrate the equity principle and sustainability factor into micro development processes. This in turn, could strengthen the bottom-up development processes with its impact on the so-called mainstream development.

Though NGOs have promoted vast social infrastructure of the poor and marginalized, the women, the dalits, adivasis, the agri-laborers etc. transforming them into reality depends very much on the political initiative of the people which, in turn, depends on the perspectives with which NGOs organize them.

The experiences of some of the NGOs in some States confirm such possibilities. Sharing of different perspectives and experiences will not only help to clarify many doubts but will also help to develop better strategies for the future to facilitate experience sharing and forge ahead in strengthening linkages and common perspectives appropriate to the local situation.

From sympathy and empathy approach and efficiency theories that led to the concept of women development, the gradual realization to improve the situation of the women, particularly the poor, to lead for positional change in the society is taking place among many NGOs, but the process is very slow and needs to be speeded up. While a large number of NGOs focus on women, women empowerment perspectives are yet to be developed in the case of the majority.

While there is increasing realization on the need to focus on the environmental concerns, internalizing the concept and promoting best practices, promoting successful and replicable models that are manageable by the people, strong micro-macro linkage and perspectives are yet to be developed with spread effects. The general environment movements need to be combined with replicable village level models.

The NGOs by-and-large focus on developmental activities at the grass-roots. In doing so, many NGOs tried to fill in the gap where government institutions and departments (like health and education) failed by running parallel programs to provide services. Such an approach has not succeeded in creating an impact on the government departments to improve the quality of services they provide. On the other hand it made the government look towards NGOs to deliver services and make the people dependent on the NGOs. The net result has been further strengthening of the dependency of the needy people. The right course would be to provide information, create awareness and strengthen the capability of the people to demand from the system and get their basic needs and services as their fundamental right.

The basic needs issue cannot be addressed and solved unless the people assert their rights and create a demand system. There is also a need in a country like India, (where political right is considered a fundamental right), to consider the basic socio-economic and cultural rights as fundamental rights. The basic needs must be seen from the basic rights perspective and grassroot development social action must be combined with legal action.

Such a perspective calls for deeper studies, analysis, experiential learning and resources development at the grassroots. The regional and national level judicial activism needs to percolate down to the village level to combine social action with legal instruments to enable the marginalized to get socio-economic justice.

The traditional form of advocacy in India has been more of social mobilization to show the strength of the poor and the marginalized. The approach of promoting successful demonstrative and replicable models (like micro-banking systems) and influencing policy is a later development. Lobbying with parliamentarians, government institutions and individuals is another method used by NGOs now and then, but not so effectively. Strong policy research, alternate models/suggestions are very much essential for policy advocacy.

Media advocacy and campaign to influence public policies and educate the public on the development issues is a recent phenomenon; compared to the complexity of the problem and vividness of the activities. However, much needs to be is done at the local level to educate the public and public institutions by using the media. Public support and solidarity is very much needed for sustained advocacy and struggle. Transparency and public accountability gives a lot of legitimacy and moral strength to face the wrong doers. NGOs are seen locally by many with suspect eyes and the people organized by them are seen as beneficiaries. The local media has to play a very important role in development education which in turn would strengthen the process of empowerment of the poor.

From the social organization concept of the late 1970s many NGOs now are involved in organizing self help groups focusing on participatory group dynamics. The activities and training imparted do not go beyond the groups. If the intervention has to lead to social transformation processes, the group dynamics should lead to a process of providing leadership to the entire communities who are poor and marginalized. While as an entry point one could focus on groups, on caste, ethnicity, gender, etc. the large forces that are constantly working against the poor and marginalized cannot be resisted without much broader unity. Therefore, sustained efforts to protect what they have and to get more in a sustainable way needs larger unity and solidarity among all those struggling for a better livelihood.

Historically, power has had three components: money, muscle and information (triad). NGOs transfer the economic leg of the triad to the focal community through various means — whether directly through an economic programme such as savings and credit or indirectly by organizing them and gaining the community access to resources. Muscle is provided through organization and access to political power.

It is the information part of the triad that has gained ascendance now. Access to data is relatively easy, but the skills to transform this into information, and put it to work in time is a demanding task. NGOs will have to fulfil this task.

Another important element is enabling rural communities to gain critical mass or 'scale'. This means exercise of power in relation to politics, economy and society. The intervention must be in a large enough area, covering a large enough population, with enough resources to be able to withstand external pressures without the external support.

The communities must achieve critical mass in terms of resources so that it is not at the mercy of the external macro-forces. This is usually done by NGOs by creating a large enough corpus fund — by enabling people say, Self Help Groups, to access formal credit systems. The most sustainable means, however, remains taking control over natural resources and the means of production.

At all times, the emphasis of NGOs should be to create a culture of self-reliance, not a culture of dependency — most of all on itself. While emphasis can be given to different sections-women, adivasi or dalits, for instance, the objective should be to unite all the poor, since their strength is their numbers. The poor should not be further divided on any account.

The number of people must be large enough since other dominant sections will gang up against any genuine restructuring of social relations. This can be done by forming broad alliances across communities, and networks among NGOs. While ethnic or racial identities such as the caste or adivasi ones can be maintained or even strengthened, it is imperative that alliances must be built up. Fragmentation of forces has been the bane of resistance movements world over, through history.

Concluding Remarks

In this subcontinent, NGOs are rendering multitudes of services and executing varied programmes such as relief, rehabilitation, income generation, community organization, awareness creation, capacity building and recently advocacying, lobbying, empowering etc. The works done by NGOs need to be truly extolled and eulogised as their foot / work prints are seen in almost all the nook and corner of the villages in the country. But observations reveal that most of the NGOs are busy involved in accomplishing soft tasks and they confine their roles to a few villages in a given area. They seem to be satisfied in working in isolation and delivering certain social services.

They need to perform many more hard tasks encountering threats and challenges so as to bring about desired rural development. They must awake themselves professionally. They need to sensitively observe and critically analyse the social, economic, commercial and political trends around the world, between nations, within the country and of their own regions. Every now and then, they need to self-assess their grass-root interventions whether they are relevant in relation to the changing world order. They have to network people's organisations and strategically ally them. So that they can protect themselves from being marginalised by external forces. Othewise, the social infrastructure created in the village level by NGOs out of their hard work for decades may be blown away by the wings of Macro/Power centres. NGOs must be conscious about the global forces and at the same time carryout their interventions relevant to the requirements of their service villages.

Several times, as an NGO person, I was asking a question myself : Why at all NGOs are needed? What is their unique role? Is it confined to giving something or doing something to the poor? The following episode gives an answer :

A baby was blown away into the river. Someone jumped inside and saved the baby. He and all the others around him felt happy. After sometime, another baby was blown away in the same way. Once again, he jumped inside and saved the baby. Still after sometime, yet another baby was blown away into the water and was saved. Like this, series of babies were blown away one after the other. Some were saved but many were lost. This is because, those who saved as well as the people aound the bank did not understand that some miscreants were throwing away the babies from the other and hidden part of the river. As they were unaware of this, they failed to stop them from doing this inhumane and antisocial activity.

NGOs' role like saving such thrown and blown away babies is quite appreciable. But facilitating a process of identifying and stopping the baby throwing elements, be it local or global, small or big, is essential.

NGOs need not confine themselves in providing temporary remedies but strive for ensuring sustainable solutions.

Whatever they do, it is the time for NGOs to think globally and then to act locally so as to ensure their intervention relevant, appropriate, latest, just and right.

2

Evolution and Growth of Voluntary Organisations

"Love finds no lock"

— *Thirukkural*
(written 2000 years back by Thiruvalluvar)

In this chapter the evolution and growth of voluntary efforts has been briefed. The influence of different religious principles on voluntary work has been incorporated. The trend of voluntary initiatives carried out during the pre and post independence era has also been highlighted.

As man is a **Gregarious Animal** Voluntarism is as old as human civilisation. Voluntarism is an inner drive among human beings, though it varies from person to person.

The term 'voluntary agencies' refers to those Non-Governmental Organisations (NGOs) which originate and function independently outside the governmental system, having service as their primary concern. In this book the term 'voluntary organisations' and 'voluntary agencies' are the synonymous terms for NGOs. The history of voluntary associations dates back to the Palaeolithic period. Since then it underwent a process of historical evolution and emerged as a concept in the twentieth century, more particularly after World War II. Missionary zeal, war and calamities, socio-economic discriminations and ideological interest are the chief attributes that promoted the growth of voluntary agencies. The ideals of welfare state, creation of world bodies, the terrible and increasing disasters both man-made and natural, ethnic riots and clash of interests have widened the sphere of voluntary organisations world wide.

Human society is a product of voluntary association influenced by environmental determinism. The voluntary agencies have a parallel evolution with the evolution of human society and its cultural matrix. Risk-management, collection of food and biological and psychological needs enforced a kind of voluntary union among the primitives. As the group was moving in search of food, common interest developed. It was further strengthened by kinship organisations. When the tribes settled down finally society was born. Thus voluntary association was the corner stone on which the whole edifice of early social action was built.

As the society advanced in technology and complexity the need for voluntary association became more pronounced. The emergence of political economy necessitated the origin of lineage kingdoms. As the lineage kingdoms became integrated into bigger states, social insurance had become the primary concern of the state. Kinship obligations, i.e., serving the kinsfolk and commitments of lineage heads began to increase. At this stage human service was more related to economic activity and social security.

With the establishment of state control over the economic resources and risk-management human service was more ascribed to the state, thus imposing an obstacle to the process of evolution of voluntary service organisations. However the kinship institutions continued to serve the local groups with reciprocal assistance. The aggressive competition for resources led to the situation of 'the war of all against all'. In such circumstances the fittest survived, while the less fit struggled to exist. It required assistance and compassion for their survival. This environmental determinism encouraged the growth of voluntary organisations.

In our country the evolutionary growth of voluntarism is clearly seen in the records of past history right from the Buddhistic times or even earlier. Examples are the Chanakya's *Arthasastra,* written around 325 B.C, the ancient Tamil Epic Silapathikaram, the epic of Anklet etc.

When the reformist religions - BUDDHISM and JAINISM, came to prominence, a new emphasis was given to human life and charities and infused the sense of moral obligations towards the weak and suffering.

The concept of dharma was integrated into the service structure of the society. These ideals were put into practice by Asoka and it can be presumed that voluntary actions had their genesis during his days. Tree seedlings were planted all along the road and ponds were dug out with the involvement of the people. So also in the olden days, temples, choultries, irrigation tanks etc., were constructed with the voluntary initiatives of the people concerned.

Christianity was founded on the sacred principle of "Love Thy Neighbour as Thyself". The teachings of Christ inspired the followers to help others like good Samaritan. Service to those of the least among humans is deemed as the service to have been done to the Almighty. It became largely accepted that serving the poor and needy was an act of Christian virtue.

Voluntary efforts in rural development were taken as systematically organised endeavours only in the 19th century. An active role in the field of rural transformation largely in the inaccessible parts of the country was played by the christian missionaries in the realm of health and education in the rural India.

The foundations for the voluntary agency movement were laid down in the pre-Independence period, some of them associated with the social reform movements of the late nineteenth century, largely concerned with educational and cultural matters and only tangentially with the question of poverty. Christian missionary groups established a network of hospitals, schools, and welfare services for the poor in the first half of the twentieth century. An yet another tradition was the Gandhian approach, which combined social reform with village development activities. A series of experiments in rural development have been tried out in different parts of the country which contributed significantly to the strategies and methodologies of introducing planned change. Poet Tagore carried out the rural reconstruction work at Silaidaha in 1908 and at Sriniketan around 1921. Spencer Hatch undertook a programme to develop the rural poor in and around Martandam under the auspices of Young Mens' Christian Association in 1929. Mahatma Gandhi initiated the Process of transformation of socio-economic life at Sevagram around 1931 based on his ideology of truth and non-violence. Jugtram Dave carried out the rural reconstruction work from the Swarajya Ashrama at Vedchi, from 1922 onwards. These and several other endeavours have significantly contributed to the principles of rural transformation through voluntary action prior to independence.

The Christian and Gandhian approaches continued to predominate after Independence. In the early post-Independence period, disaster relief and food-for-work programmes came to be associated with Christian organizations in particular. Welfare/Charity approach was dominant in voluntary agencies in the 1950s and early 1960s. Agencies steeped in Gandhian values emphasized village self-reliance and provided the foundation for development activities centred on small-scale agriculture and cottage industry. The community development approach became popular in the late 1960s, and early 1970s, with NGOs combining health and education with economic programmes in pursuit of poverty alleviation. It was also at this time that funding from international NGOs began to make its mark.

During the latter half of the 1970s, community organisation gained momentum. Also a radical trend emerged, with social action groups taking the view that poverty was a structural phenomenon which had to be tackled head-on through the active mobilization of the rural poor. They abjured violence but the thrust of their activities was confrontational, initiating struggles over issues such as land reform, wages, and bonded labour, while another dimension of their work rested on empowering the poor to demand efficient delivery of services from the state and pressing for the implementation of progressive componenets of government legislation. With liberal foreign funding, social action groups proliferated throughout the late 1970s and early 1980s, and established themselves as the dominant type of NGO in some States, notably Tamil Nadu and Bihar, in sharp contrast to the Programme-focused approaches which had found favour from the 1960s (Unia, 1991). By the mid - 1980s, however, their relatively limited economic achievements led to a questioning of the basic tenets of this approach. At the same time, there was growing criticism of the lack of participation by the poor in the design and implementation of NGO development programmes.

From the mid-1980s, a further trend emerged within the NGO movement, emphasizing the importance of a professional approach based on sound management, planning, and co-ordination. People's participation in development was much pronounced in 1980s. A parallel development was the creation of resource agencies which work directly with the poor and also provide support services to other NGOs in the form of training, evaluation, and documentation. These agencies are usually financed by core grants from foreign donors and payments for staff training from individual NGOs. Intermediary agencies responsible for channelling funds from foreign donors to small national NGOs in some cases also provide these types of services, for example, in assisting in evaluations.

There has been an element of convergence between these various approaches, with NGOs seeking to combine project-specific development work with active organization of the poor. Reflecting this greater uniformity, community organization is now treated, for the most part, as an essential prerequisite of the successful introduction and implementation of specific programmes. Similarly, most NGOs now recognize that organizational work among the poor cannot be sustained without material improvements derived from programme-specific activities.

Many NGOs work through local groups, though with considerable variation in purpose and approach. Some, notably the Gandhian agencies, chose to work through existing village institutions (panchayats or gram sabhas). But these are invariably dominated by the rural elite, and most NGOs therefore prefer to form groups which exclude the wealthier members of the village community. In some cases, caste or tribal affiliations constitute the basis for group formation, while others, particularly the social action groups, restrict their membership to the landless or marginal farmers. Another approach is to include all the poor, irrespective of caste or class. In some cases membership is defined by a common occupation, such as farming or fishing.

In 1990s empowerment approach has started to gain momentum. NGOs began to perform advocacying and lobbying in order to meet the challenges and threats of macro forces towards the rural poor and marginalised.

As NGOs have grown in size and influence, their activities have brought them into closer contact with the Government. The NGOs are recognised by the Government in rural reconstruction work. They received explicit recognition from the Government in the latter half of 1980s. The Seventh Five Year Plan (1986 - 1990) emphasised the involvement of voluntary agencies in various proposed projects. The eighth plan further added credits to NGOs and encouraged them to participate in the innovative projects like Agro Climatic Regional Planning (ACRP), the watershed development project under DPAP etc. The Nineth Plan envisaged to involve NGOs right from the Planning Process. In 1999 the SGSY scheme has been launched merging various rural development schemes like IRDP, JRY etc., Group - lending remains the major thrust. As NGOs have done pioneering work in SHG promotion they are being extensively involved in influencing the SHGs.

NGOs receive foreign funds for a variety of rural projects. The total inflow of foreign funds is estimated more than Rs. 800 crores every year.

Concluding Remarks

Voluntary organisations have become an integral part of rural development. Voluntary efforts initiated more as a charity in earlier days have now become a full-fledged professional intervention. Hope Voluntary organisations will work with a wider vision, professional wisdom and profound will and bring about a "better future society" in the forth-coming years.

3

Theory of Voluntarisms

Love thy neighbour as thyself

— *Holy Bible*

This chapter deals with the theory of voluntarisms that are prevalent among individuals. Over the 22 years of my personal involvement with NGOs, researches, observations analyses and listening to spokesmen, I have made an attempt to propound a theory of voluntarisms. In fact, voluntary organisations are the outcome and manifestations of such voluntarism. NGOs are promoted chiefly by one or a few persons supported by a group of like minded persons who have similar inspirations. Individuals make the organisation. If individuals are good organisations will naturally be good. This innate inspiration, a missionary zeal, inner drive, humanitarian concern, love for others, a divine or a social calling realised within an individual, a burden within one's heart to serve others, helping thirst, etc., gain the shape of voluntarism.

Such inspirations are derived from religious doctrines or societal demands. Also, voluntarism within a person is enhanced and influenced by great social thinkers and reformers like Mahatma Gandhi, Jaya Prakash Narain, Karl Marx, Dr. Ambedkar, Mother Terasa etc.

Education of certain disciplines like Social Work, Community Development, Social Dynamics, Sociology, Liberation Theology etc., also concretise the voluntarism of individuals who later on practise the same in a more professional manner. In certain cases, deep frustration and extreme grief in individuals turn them to become committed social workers.

It cannot be denied that, sometimes, the need for survival of the jobless and on some other occasions, the lust for money give rise to an **artificial voluntarism** among individuals.

Birds of the same feather flock together. Similarly people of similar category of voluntary inspirations join together.

Let us now proceed to analyse the theory of voluntarisms which describes the various categories of voluntarisms one by one.

THEORY OF VOLUNTARISMS

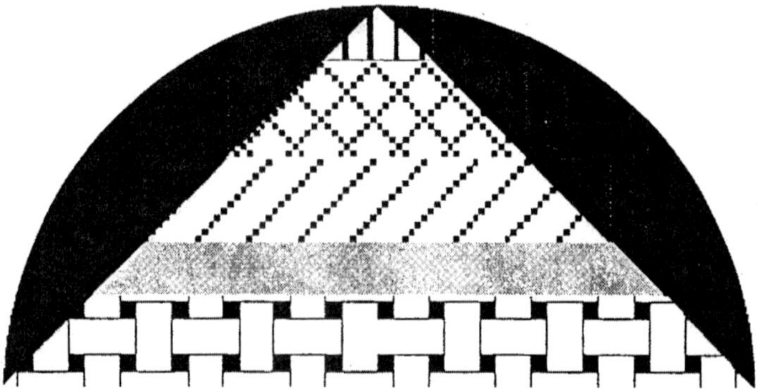

CATEGORY WISE

	Roughly
Sacrificial Voluntarism	Hardly 1%
Professional voluntarism	10% to 15%
Amateur/Xerox Copy Voluntarism	20% to 25%
Ventilatory Voluntarism	5% to 10%
Survival Voluntarism	25% to 30%
Pseudo Voluntarism	25% to 35%

1. SACRIFICIAL VOLUNTARISM

People with this spirit of voluntarism will strive to work for the uplift of the poor, oppressed, neglected and marginalised unto the last. They have clear "vision" and they dedicate their life itself as the means to accomplish the same. They continue to render their yeoman services altruistically under any threats and crises. They live for others and are even prepared to sacrifice themselves for a noble cause. Persons like Mahatma Gandhi, Mother Teresa, Dr. Ambedkar *et al.* can be enlisted under such category. There are many others in the country whose names might not have been made popular nor do they wish so. Such persons bestowed with this kind of voluntarism may be honoured as the salt and the light of the earth. They are mostly none but born volunteers. In some cases such people emerge in the course of their life experiences. High thinking and simple living are their principles. They have strong will and profound commitment. Even death cannot threaten their voluntarism. They are the crusadors of the oppressed and unprivileged. They need not go to colleges or universities to learn the theories of voluntarism. Infact, theories of voluntary work are evolved out of their experiences and impact created. They can bring about social transformation and changes in government policies in favour of the depressed. People follow them as their leaders or Gurus (teachers) and extend their support for their mission and still a few may even become disciples. They maintain a soul-to-soul rapport with the suffering and strive for their uplift. They are the personification of altruism. They are hardly 1%. However, it becomes difficult for their successors to sustain the same wave-length of voluntarism.

The disadvantage is that this kind of voluntarism fades, dwindles and even perishes along with such great people if the followers do not carry on the work with the similar spirit.

2. PROFESSIONAL AND DEVELOPMENTAL VOLUNTARISM

They are clear in the concept of development. They are aware of the vision and mission of the organisation and execute the programmes with clear objective and appropriate strategies. Persons working in agencies like CASA, CARE, MYRADA, ASSEFA etc. are the examples. Persons of this category are endowed with professional competence on one side and commitment on the other. Such people are prepared to forego monetary benefits for the cause of social objectives. They firmly believe that people's development lies in people's hands. They are not mere doers but facilitators. Their work is people - centred and process oriented. They are gender - sensitive. Class, caste and gender concepts are inter-woven in their dealings only 10 to 15% of such people are seen in NGO sector.

Their interventions are pivoted on capacity-building of the people and hence they create sustainable people's organisations, programmes and systems.

In some developmental organisations, it is observed that there are two categories of people - one, the traditional bureaucrats, (i.e.) the power mongers and the other, charismatic personalities, (i.e.) the professionalists and active workers. Seniority is the only criteria of the former while sincerity is the latter's. The charismatic people, while frustrated tend to get out of organisations to float new agencies with professionalism.

3. AMATEUR VOLUNTARISM/XEROX COPY VOLUNTARISM

Persons who have concern for others but devoid of professional code and ethics may be enlisted under this category. They wish to do something for others. They think that doing anything for others is development work and they function as raw development workers. This is because they are inexperienced and untrained. They believe mostly in social service, relief and charity. On seeing other NGOs, they misconceive that it is very easy to run an organisation. They do not have original thoughts of their own nor any vision or mission or strategy. They simply xerox-copy the other NGOs. Some copy the good and some others bad. In some cases, the initial interventions may seem to be brighter. But in the long run, they fade away. In some other cases, their role is unclear, vague, inferior invisible and unseen. In certain exceptional cases, copying social workers do better than the meek originals. The presence of this kind of people in voluntary sector would be between 20 and 25 per cent. They become susceptible to external forces and vulnerable to threats. Such organisations governed by amateur voluntarism may tend to be constituency driven and donor driven and not the mission driven ones.

4. VENTILATORY VOLUNTARISM

Elites, opulents and business magnates who are also interested in the welfare of the depressed and poor fall under this category. Examples are persons like Lions , Rotarians, Tablers etc. Their services are, no doubt, welcome and deserve appreciation though theirs are hobby like activities. They go from the towns to the nearby accessible villages during their leisure or holidays and conduct health camps, supply medicines free of cost and give charities to the poor. Their activities are expression of their kindness towards others. Thus they ventilate their urban stresses and so also fulfil their social obligations. They are bet 5 and 10 per cent among the voluntory workers. Usually they opproach the media for coverage. Sometimes the advertisement will be more than their accomplishments.

With their resources, they can do wonders and bring about a social change, if they have separate development wings monitored by developmentalists. But there is no continuity and sustainability of their programmes. Theirs are sudden interventions with cheers and quick withdrawal owing to their own day-to-day pressures. They require orientation on people centred development.

5. SURVIVAL VOLUNTARISM

Voluntary work becomes primarily a bread-winning profession for this category of people. Less committed, less motivated, less devoted, less qualified and myopic visioned come under this section. Voluntary organisations are promoted and utilised more for their existence than for the commonwealth of the weaker sections. They are not very much concerned about the ideologies, principles, philosophy and concepts of development nor are they very much bothered to learn them. They are curious in mobilising resources for their subsistence.

They stoop down before resource agencies unmindful of the needs of thc constituencies. Hay or Clay, they will happily receive from the resource agencies without any clarification. To quote they would undertake projects on gobar gas and construct the plants for all the families of a village including those who do not have animals at all. This is being done just because money is made available for such programmes. They may justify that the beneficiaries would be granted loans for cattle under SGSY in the ensuing year and afterwards their gobargas plants will be put into use. In simple words, development becomes a social drama for them. Sometimes the drama may be thematic. Such groups shift their development tents from village to village or region to region in accordance with the availability of the resources.

For them voluntarism is not deep rooted but resource oriented. When serious challenges or threats are faced by them such categories would relinquish voluntary work and create alternative source of livelihood like establishing petty business or trades. Being money centred they are even prepared to lose the chastity of the organisation for obtaining a charity from resource agency. In the long run most of them will tend to turn down to the category of anti voluntarism or pseudo voluntarism while a few may change towards positive paths.

It is unfortunate that in this country 25 to 30 per cent of today's so called NGOs fall under this category. NGOs mushroom and proliferate for their survival. This category needs to be set right, mended, repaired, modified or severely dealt with so that voluntary sector could be protected from being handled by inferior, selfish and anti-social personalities. Resource providers and the regulating authorities are required to play a just and judicious role in this regard. If, so they can be corrected.

6. PSEUDO VOLUNTARISM

People of this category start NGOs with a deliberate motive of amassing money by misusing the good banner of voluntary organisation. This is the growing problem of today in the NGO sector. People have started thinking that voluntary agencies are the easiest means for making money. The expelled staff of NGOs, unemployed graduates, retired officials, the businessmen, traders, industrialists, religious leaders, politicians etc. tend to consider that NGOs are the risk free short cut means to become rich overnight and hence they register some voluntary organisations. Their agencies may be indicated as Letter-pad NGOs, Name board NGOs, Money making institutions, Family Trust for evasion of tax, Private Enterprises in Public Clothing, Pseudo institutions, Social Contractors, Social parasites, Wolves in sheep-skin NGOs, Project Brokers, Development Assassinators etc.

The availability of funds, both abroad and within the country, have succumbed to the growth of such organisations. The government departments are being increasingly instructed to implement the programmes through NGOs but it is a developmental tragedy and social malady that pseudo NGOs and some resource agents have become hand in glove to work out their shares. The programme implementation by such NGOs becomes a social tresspass. Carrying a handbag full of currency to funding agencies and collecting back a suitcase full of money to their voluntary agencies under the pretext of people's development has become a stealthy practice of the pseudo NGOs. They adopt hook and crook methods and even immoral endeavours to entice the funding representatives. It is inferior to state that 'Wine and Women' too are involved in the gambling of securing funds for the so called voluntary organisations. It is misfortunate that around 30 per cent is encroached by pseudoes.

The emergence and proliferation of pseudo organisations have become a great threat to voluntary sector. Pseudo NGO persons need to be penalised and their NGOs should be scraped out.

I perceive that around 500 NGOs are being born along with the sunrise. So also 500 die along with sunset. To my understanding atleast one NGO is registered every day in each district of India. What is the reason?

On various occasions, I have come across persons who made pungent remarks on NGOs. Once a core team [including me] was representing a group of 150 NGOs to a district collector to undertake a District level project on a collective basis. The first question he asked was that how many of the NGOs are 'BAD'.

Somehow, we convinced the District collector and got the project approved. Even then the project serious and series of prolems before accomplishments. Not only District collectors, many others like academics, Government officials, Bankers, and common public too make fun of NGOs. This attitude of generalising all NGO persons as bad needs to be rooted out.

Something must be done. Some transformation must emerge from NGOs.

NGOs sector is seen bad not just because of the bad activities of bad NGOs but also because of the insensitivity and inactivities of good NGOs in responding together.

To quote farmers produce paddy and deliver the same to the society. Is it not their responsibility to pluck off the weeds during the process of cultivation? Otherwise weeds will crush away the plants. Similarly if the same trend continues, bad NGOs will suppress the good ones and NGO movement will be in peril. Whether some one has to come for the rescue of NGOs from NGOs' oppression?

Hence NGOs ought to together act diligently and protect the NGO sector as a part of their development intervention. NGOs need to be transparent as they work for the public welfare and common weal. Good NGOs must carryout collective action not only to address social problems but also to rectify their own sectoral problems. If NGOs can not work together [who advocate people's organisations to act together] it means they are either weak in their will or their priority is their own priority than social transformation.

The major reason for growing pseudo voluntarism is the availability of money as aid/grant from funding sources. Industrialists or businessmen invest and produce quality products and supply the same to customers. The survival and growth of them depends purely upon the customers with whom they deal with. Either manufacturing or service industries, they are directly answerable to the customers or clients. If the customers are dissatisfied, they will be naturally thrown out of the business. What is quality? It is the 'degree or level of excellence' or "something that is special in a person or thing".

Customers satisfaction and quality of products/services go hand in hand. Hence industries, firms business enterprises etc. have to necessarily operate 'customers centred'.

But in NGO sector, money comes from one set of people i.e. Donars and services are delivered to another set of people i.e. Target people/Beneficieries. Funding agencies are at the giving end and NGOs are at the receiving end. In turn NGOs become givers and people as simple receivers. Beneficiaries unlike customers are not in a position to demand quality of services from NGOs as the former are already poverty striken and helpless. Hence there exists a tendency among NGOs to fulfil the requirements of money providers than the people. Funding agencies also do not monitor NGOs on day to day basis. Hence if the cause of inferior practices is attributed to the nature of voluntarism within the NGO personnel, the root cause is the bad system or inferior system of funding. A contaminated fountain can not provide potable drinking water to the people so also the polluted channels and systems of pipelines.

Hence I would advocate "system transformation" in the NGO sector in the entire project or development cycle right from planning to evaluation and funding to impact assessment.

The "culture of quality" must be inculcated among NGOs. Just because NGOs work with poor people, their services also need not be poor. Quality of service/performance/facilitation must become the centrality of their intervention. Quality is community organisation, quality in conducting meetings, quality communication, quality in training programmes, quality information dissemination, enabling quality products in IGPs, quality administration and management, quality documentation etc. need to become the order of the 21st century NGOs. This quality culture must percolate down to the people's organisations as an impact of NGOs' intervention. As Japanese use Kaizan technique in management, continuous improvement must be there in NGO field. Then only true community development and transformation will take place.

In sacrificial and professional voluntarism, quality of performance is in built. Sacrificial voluntarism is most preferred. But it is seldom is available. Professional voluntarism is and, if not, can be made available by continuous training and motivation. NGO persons work for and with ordinary people but they are supposed to be extraordinary people with something special in them and in their intervention.

7. TRANSFIGURATION OF VOLUNTARISM

The aforesaid six types of voluntarisms [Other than the sixth category (i.e.) pseudo voluntarism] may chance to transfigure to one another upward or downward in the course of their experience and involvement with the communities. For example, persons of amateur voluntarism may gain professional competence and perform the functions of well organised developmental organisation, whereas the members of developmental organisation due to lack of good motivation and orientation or sometimes due to ill-treatment by their bosses may tend to perform their activities ill professional and they may even turn down to pseudo workers.

Hence organisations need to keep the voluntary workers with high motivation and good morale for which the human resource development programmes within the organisations must be given utmost importance. It is the bound and duty of each voluntary worker and organisation to see that more and more NGO persons move upward towards professional and sacrificial voluntarism and there shall be no space for pseudoes.

Concluding Remarks

If true Voluntarism is expressed in actions, that are known as voluntary actions.

If voluntary actions are carried out in an organised manner by a group of like minded individuals that would be called voluntary organisations.

If organisations carry out activities blended with zealous voluntarism and quality in built professionalism then, they will be named as "Genuine Voluntary Organisations".

4

Framework and Types of NGOs

In this chapter the definition and meaning of NGOs, the Organisational Vision, Mission and Strategies are discussed. Followed by that the different types of NGOs and the parameters of classifications are also described.

1. DEFINITION AND MEANING

It is not easy to define voluntary organisation in a simple definition. But we can describe the same its characteristics, types and functions. Two definitions have been given below which give an overall view of voluntary organisation.

A voluntary organisation is a social service and developmental institution motivated to meet the needs of the most disadvantaged in society, either through direct services to the people or through facilitative/ indirect services to other voluntary organisations or Government, non-profit making and not undertaken to be fully funded for its maintenance, directly or indirectly by the Government. (Drawn in the National Conference on the Role of Voluntary Organisation in Health Care in India).

Voluntary Organisations are non-profit making agencies that are constituted with a vision by a group of like minded people, committed for the uplift of the poor, marginalised, unprivileged, underprivileged, impoverished, downtrodden and the needy and they are closer and accessible to the target groups, flexible in administration, quicker in decision making, timely in action and facilitating the people towards self-reliance ensuring their fullest participation in the whole process of development.

2. CHARACTERISTICS AND SPECIALITIES OF NGOS

(i) **Voluntary :** They are formed voluntarily. There is an element of voluntary involvement in the organisation. NGOs are built upon commitment of a few persons.

(ii) **Legal Status :** NGOs are registered with the Government under the Societies Act, Trust Act and a few under Trade Union Act etc.

NGOs are also registered under Foreign Contribution Regulation Act (FCRA) with the Ministry of Home Affairs, Government of India. This is to get entitled for obtaining funds abroad.

(iii) **Independent :** NGOs are independent in planning and implementation of their programmes. They are not bound by the hard and fast rules as in Government institution.

(iv) **Flexible :** NGOs are flexible in interventions. They are not bound by red tapism and bureaucratic obstacles. In the name of audit objections, they won't cease people's initiatives.

(v) **Quicker in decision-making :** NGOs take quick decisions in response to the needs of the community. As decisions are taken quickly, their services are delivered timely to the people. NGOs could overcome the constraints of cumbersome procedures and act readily to the community demands.

(vi) **Non-Profit Oriented :** NGOs are not run on profit motives. The surplus and gains from economic projects, if any, are not distributed to the members or stake holders. They are re-used for development purposes.

(vii) **Not Self-serving:** NGOs are constituted not for the benefit of the promoters. NGOs serve the poor and impoverished for their upliftment and not for that of NGOs themselves. The NGO members are nurtured by the response and co-operation of the people. This offers a great deal of mental satisfaction to the NGO members which inspires them to do better and more.

(viii) **High Motivation :** The members and the staff are endowed with high motivation and inspiration to work for the cause of the poor. Their hours of work are not clock bound. They strive tirelessly to achieve their purpose for the benefit of the target groups.

(ix) **Freedom in work :** NGO workers enjoy their maximum freedom in their field work, in organising the community and carrying out the development schemes. Such freedom becomes a source of motivation to accomplish the task inspite of their less rumeration. They are not pinched by their bosses for petty mistakes.

(x) **Value driven :** NGOs are driven by social values and humanitarian principles and hence they try to promote a value based society.

(xi) **Catalystic :** NGOs facilitate the communities towards social actions but they do not dilute and distort themselves in the process of intervention.

(xii) **People-centred :** People are the heart of the NGOs. They plan things with the people and implement the same through the people. Thus they learn the best from the people and replicate the same with other groups.

3. CONCEPTUALISATION OF THE TERM — 'NGO'

People in voluntary sector quite often come across a debate on how to mean a voluntary organisation. *By and large, the acronym (the short or abbreviated form) "NGO" which means Non-Governmental Organisation is being popularly used.* Many feel that there is a contradiction between the term NGOs and Voluntary Organisations since all organisations including recreation clubs, business clubs etc. having no activism or social objectives, other than Governmental, are put into the same basket of NGOs. This is true in its broader sense. But the definition of NGOs refers specifically to voluntary organisations only.

When voluntary workers meet in a training, seminar or conference they happen to argue with one another that the term **'voluntary'** must be prefixed to agency or organisation without which the identity of voluntary Organisation is lost.

In fact everyone can verily accept the term 'Voluntary' which offers an explitcit sense to refer to voluntary organisation. But in practice, the word NGO has been much more used in all contexts by the U.N. Organisations, World Bank, Funding Agencies abroad, the Resource agencies within the country, various Government departments, writers and even by voluntary agencies themselves. Of late, the term 'Voluntary Development Organisation' is being used.

Hence, in this book the term 'NGO' is synonymous to Voluntary Organisations having people's Development as their primary objective and being endowed with other characteristics as stated above.

4. ORGANIZATIONAL "VISION"

In the words of Dr. Alan Fowler, an organization's vision is its view of how it would perceive the world to be, its hopes for "**reality to be**" as opposed to the "**reality that is**". Visions are expressions of ideals, and may not be attainable in one lifetime or even in many lifetimes.

Organizational visions often originate from an individual vision founder, or from a group of people who have some ideas about how life could be made better than what it actually is. These ideas may spring forth from personal experience or from a religious or ideological source. Whatever the source may be, visions are the lifeblood of effective development organizations in several ways.

A shared vision is often the initial force that brings people together for collective action. People with visions of social or political transformation frequently decide that they must join with others who share their vision. If they have any hope of attaining it, they can join the existing organizations or start a new one. Once joined together in an organization, the members may re-examine or redefine their individual visions until a truly shared or collective one emerges. It is usually the role of the vision founder or founders' group to ensure that the vision is kept alive, and stated in a way that it may be broadly shared by other organization members.

Shared visions are vitally important throughout the life of a development organization. Voluntary development work is often difficult, poorly paid, personally threatening, and results are sometimes invisible. A clearly articulated vision can provide energy, momentum and strength to individuals working in development organizations and can be a continuing focus for their social commitment. A shared vision can also help bind an organization together in times of crises, and provides the incentive to work amidst internal conflicts.

5. ORGANIZATIONAL MISSION

A statement of organizational mission describes the organization's purpose for existing, given the vision of the "reality to be." It describes in general terms how the vision is to be pursued. For example, one organization whose vision is to create "a world where no child ever dies of a preventable disease," has as its mission "to reduce infant mortality by providing health services to women and children in underserved areas." Another organization with the same vision, might choose as its mission to "engage in social mobilization to change the economic conditions which foster malnutrition and disease."

A clear mission connects the vision to a method for achieving that vision, and this has a number of benefits. A clear mission can guide an organization's leaders in major policy decisions about alternative courses of action. It helps define both what the organization will do and what it will not do. If broadly understood and shared, the mission helps collective action in a common direction, so that peoples' energy and organizations' resources serve a common purpose. Otherwise, even people with a shared vision may propose individual paths to the vision and the power of collective action would be lost. For people working on day-to-day operations, a shared mission may provide meaning and motivation since it can help them see how their work contributes to attainment of the vision.

The mission is the starting point for keeping an organization focused and effective. A shared mission functions like a compass, bringing the organization back on course despite constantly changing demands from constituents, and political and economic forces.

As with the vision, it is usually the role of an organization's leaders to articulate the mission and help others understand it. Formulating the Mission with the involvement of organization staff, board members, and other constituents can be an effective way of building joint ownership of the same.

Only rarely, and usually after extreme organizational tension and pain, will an organization change its vision. Changing mission is also a major shock to an organization, and is a relatively unusual event. However, if there has been a big change in an organization's analysis of development problems, political space, or other constituent demands, re-examination of organization mission may be in order. A change in strategy is often sufficient to keep an organization effective, even in the face of major shifts in its external context. But unless the mission is occasionally tested against an analysis of the current situation, the organization could cease to be an effective instrument for realizing the vision.

For the reference of the readers the Vision and Mission of CASA (A popular voluntary organization in India) is given here.

Vision of CASA

CASA's Vision is inspired by the Christian Faith and Values. CASA visualizes a society in which peace, justice and equality prevail and wherein all citizens - irrespective of caste, creed, language and religion — live in peace and communal harmony. CASA also envisages a society where the poor, the marginalised and the under-privileged have equal opportunity for their involvement in the development process which is value based and sustainable, and also have an appropriate environment to develop their fullest potential.

Mission of CASA

CASA actively supports and works towards a just and sustainable society by creating conditions for meaningful and disciplined involvement of all people and their organisations, in the development process which is based on macro approach and involves networking of the organisations at various appropriate levels. CASA also responds to human suffering and distress caused by natural or man-made calamities, in a manner which upholds the dignity of the affected people and enhances their capacity for disaster mitigation and management of the programmes which are in accordance with development principles. In doing all this, CASA strives to optimise all potential from within the organisation, as well as, its reference community and other partner organisations.

6. THE STRATEGY

Once the mission is clearly articulated and explicitly stated then the need arises to elaborate how the organisations are going to accomplish it.

This means that there is a need to spell out the strategy which is appropriate for moving in the directions set by the mission.

A strategy is a set of concepts that guide an organization's use of its resources to pursue its mission.

The same resources can be used in many different ways to address development problems. As is true of organization's mission, choice of strategy will also depend in large part on the organization's social change theory, and on its analysis of the problem and of contextual forces and trends. An accurate analysis and theory of social change should help identify leverage points where organization activity will have the most impact. Organizations that are very ideologically driven must be careful that the purity of the ideology does not limit their strategic options, and result in reflective or irrelevant strategies. For example, an ideological belief that social mobilization for advocacy is the only way to address development problems may blind an organization to the possibility that non-formal education could be a valuable aspect of their strategy.

Embedded in a stragegy are answers to the questions:

What is the nature of the development problems the organization seeks to solve ?

How will the activities of the organization contribute to substantial and sustainable change in those problems?

How can the organization use its strengths and avoid its weaknesses to accomplish its mission? and so on.

Strategy and Day to Day Programme Operations

Most importantly, strategy provides concepts that guide choices about:

1. **What to do.** Strategy allows decisions about where and how to use scarce resources (time, money, people) for maximum impact towards accomplishing the organization's mission.

2. **What not to do.** The organization should avoid activities that :

require more people, time, skills or funds than it is available,
will not produce results because of external constraints (such as government repression or lack of popular support),
will have no sustainable impact,
will drain energies away from central concerns, or
for other reasons will not advance the organizations' mission.

All organizations have characteristic ways of using their resources, whether or not this "strategy" is ever explicitly stated. Some organizations may be successful in achieving their missions without an explicit strategy, but most will not. Changes in the problem, or in the external context or in the organization's abilities may make old programmes and activities sirrelevant to new situations.

Once the strategies are designed the goals to be achieved, programmes to be carried out and the roles of the staff to be performed will be formulated.

To epitomise, Vision and Mission need to be explicitly articulated and shared. Strategies have also to be clearly designed and apprised to the members of NGOs. Based on that, programmes and activities could be proposed and implemented. There must be a spiral linkage from vision to activities. Visionless and Missionless organisations will tend to get involved in any kind of programmes driven by external forces. On some occasions, they may fly up or down or dive like paper - kites in the sky carried away by the winds. But sooner or later, they will disappear from the scene. Paper-kites do not know where from they start and what their destination is? In the same manner, visionless/missionless NGOs will run away from the Voluntary sector leaving disappointments to the people.

Vision is the theory of change for the organisation. Mission is the means to achieve the vision. Strategies are the guiding concepts on what to do and what not do in terms of resources.

So all the members of NGOs need to realise the significance of shared vision, mission and also the strategies and internalise them so that the focus of the organisation remain focussed.

7. TYPES OF NGOS

The functions of NGOs are varied in accordance with the programmes they undertake. Keeping in view the various activities NGOs may be classified into the following types

7.1 Charity NGOs

Charity is the earliest function of the NGOs : **Giving something to others is their primary motto.** (e.g.) Offering food, dress to the orphans and destitute, etc. Most of them believe that giving something to the poor is like giving the same to God. Their activities are transitory in nature.

7.2 Relief and Rehabilitation NGOs

NGOs who are involved in providing relief and rehabilitation programmes fall under this type. Followed by natural calamities like flood, fire or epidemic diseases or by man-made catastrophe like war, genocide etc., relief and rehabilitation services are provided by the NGOs. Supply of food packets to the flood marooned or to the victims of fire accident, health services to the ailing, rescue operations, etc. are provided by such NGOs directly or in collaboration with the Government authority.

In fact, many organisations emerge into the NGO — Sector followed by the demand for relief operations. The earthquake in Latur region (Maharashtra, India 1993) is a classic example which aroused many new NGOs on the one hand and called existings ones for their effective performance mobilising enormous resources, inside and outside the country, to meet the irrepairable loss on the other hand. Some NGOs undertake house construction for the victims and thereby ensure rehabilitation of the affected.

7.3 Service Providing NGOs

Service providing NGOs are welfare oriented. These are inspired by welfare concerns and they largely provide services for the poor and marginalised such as mobile clinics, hospitals, schools, training programmes, non-formal education, literacy, etc. They provide these services with great sacrifice, with high efficiency, with low expenses, with commitment and dedication. These services are flexible to be responsive to the needs of the community. Such service-oriented NGOs operate in those areas where government programmes are inadequate or non-existent.

A related category of welfare work is that which arises in situations requiring relief and rehabilitation, the work with refugees, the work in situations of great crises and disasters, cyclones, famine, wars, etc. The debate seems to indicate that in recent years most NGOs which started with a service and welfare orientation seem not to get limited to that but see it as a means to the wider focus of development work.

7.4 Economic Development NGOs

This type of NGOs believe that rise in income of the poor and the marginalised will bring about development for them. **Economic gain is the social gain according to them**. Hence these NGOs endeavour to provide employment opportunities to the farmers and women to mitigate poverty. They implement various income generating projects mobilising resources from the Government and the funding agencies abroad. Scientific and appropriate technologies are introduced to increase production and productivity so as to ensure more remuneration or wages to the denied.

But these NGOs are predominantly project holders while the people are their paid labourers-cum-beneficiaries. They try to uplift Dhalits, women and the oppressed by providing increased opportunities to fetch better income. These NGOs do not involve in challenging social injustice. They will be more of pro Government and pro existing systems. But within the boundry or under a given situation they want to uplift the poor.

7.5 Social Development NGOs

This type of NGOs focus more on social facets of the community. They believe that social awareness and people's involvement will bring about development. They lay more emphasis on people's component in the development programmes. They organise communities and impart social education. They sensitise and concientize people and enable them to deal with their issues. They enhance people's management in all the economic development projects and promote people's leadership.

They ensure people's participation in the process of development. However they work in isolation in a given region or cluster without much interacting with the other allied communities and NGOs.

7.6 Empowerment NGOs

These NGOs enable people to gain power and authority so that they access and control over resources.

They directly work on the question of community organisation and empowerment through educational interventions. These NGOs have begun to address a variety of development concerns-like drinking water, economic activities, literacy, adult and non-formal education and social issues against poverty, injustice etc. These are the popular education NGOs who have contributed towards development of many innovative approaches to strengthen socio-economic status of the poor and the deprived. Their approaches towards planning, interventions in socio-economic programming etc. have been very innovative, flexible and impactful. As a result, in many countries the ideas derived from the work of such NGOs have been attempted to be utilised in national policies. It is here that the work of such NGOs became the basis for formulation of national and international policies and programmes to be people centred. The work of many NGOs in the area of literacy and adult and non-formal education has become a model for many national campaigns and other national programmes.

Many of these NGOs start with a development intervention, and then build strategies for organising and empowering the people. Some others seem to start by bringing people together on issues of common concerns, conscientising and empowering them through a process of reflection and struggle and then building on development interventions and initiatives for their regeneration and sustenance.

In fact, they try to enhance powerless to become powerful. They adopt macro approach to promote people's solidarity and cohesiveness. They attempt to influence Government policy in favour of the poor and downtrodden. They play the role of advocacy and facilitate people's movement.

7.7 Network NGOs

It is interesting that the 80's also marked the rise of networks of NGOs, and umbrella or federation type of NGOs. The networks are more informal, with limited purpose and, therefore, time-bound associations of NGOs come together to work on a common issue or concern (like watershed development, Indegenous medicine, drug abuse, womens' rights, occupational health, etc.). Umbrella NGOs or federations are more formal attempts of linking NGOs together. Such networks and umbrella NGOs operating at State or national levels have emerged. The main reason for their emergence and continuance is the need for bringing together the experiences in different micro settings to address an issue that requires collective strength, advocacy and wider perspective. Thus many of these umbrella NGOs have begun to play an important role in raising the issues to the level of national and international policy debate and to contribute towards changing the frameworks and strategies of development based on the experiences of grass-roots NGOs operating in local settings.

7.8 Support NGOs

These are the newly emerging NGOs which provide a variety of support functions to different grass-root NGOs. The support functions vary depending on whether it is related to a sector (like health or education or forestry) or a general support. The work of these support institutions has been to provide inputs that would strengthen the capacities of grass-root NGOs to function more effectively and impactfully. The work of support institutions, therefore, is comprised of training, evaluation, programme planning etc.

Newness of this category of NGOs makes it rather difficult for their work to be recognised or their impact to be assessed. They contribute towards the strengthening of the work of grass-root NGOs and also those of people's organisations and social movements by extending the kinds of support which is otherwise not available to them. In broad terms, this could be defined as educational support, and not financial support, though the latter may also, in some occasions, be part of the overall package.

They provide conceptual clarity and professional and philosophical inputs to the grass root NGOs. They open the eyes of the NGOs to see their retrospects & prospects. While the NGOs bring about empowerment among the people, the support NGOs are empowering those NGOs themselves.

There are few in the country like PRIA (Participatory Research in Asia) New Delhi, ISI (Indian Social Institute) New Delhi etc.

8. MIXED ROLES

So far, we have seen 8 broad types of NGOs. But one cannot strictly say that NGOs come under any one of the particular types alone. In practice the roles of NGOs are mixed and heterogenous. An NGO involved in empowerment may also carry out economic development programmes and even relief activities during calamities. But their major focus may be confined to any one type.

9. PARAMETERS OF CLASSIFICATION

An expert team (Sponsored by PRIA, N. Delhi) which studied NGOs' roles identified the following three parameters that distinguish, in some significant ways, the voluntary organisations existing in the country today.

9.1 Inspiration

One of the most important source of differentiation in voluntary organisations is the nature of the inspiration of the Founder(s). This inspiration provides the philosophical perspective as well as an analytical framework in viewing the social reality and thereby becomes the basis for evolving a set of actions by a given voluntary organisation. The inspiration takes various forms, it may be philosophical, intellectual, religious or ideological. Different inspirations have quite different implications for the manner in which these organisations get established and the manner in which they function. Some of the common types of inspiration are described below.

Historcially, one of the most significant inspirations has been the Gandhian School built on the experience of the freedom struggle and Gandhi's call for constructive social work, to help the rural masses achieve their own economic, social and moral regeneration. Gandhian inspired voluntary organisations practise a set of norms and values in the conduct of the organisation and design certain specific targets and strategies for themselves. The keystone of such organisations has been village reconstruction - to re-establish traditional handicraft industries and create pride in 'swadeshi' or Indianness.

A second school, also historically quite active, is what could be called a socialist school. This inspiration can be best typified in the leadership of Purushottam Das Tandon, Ram Manohar Lohia and Jaya Prakash Narayan. The influence of this inspiration can be seen in the waves of voluntary organisations which emerged out of the political struggle, student movement, etc. Chhatra Yuva Sangharsh Vahini, as an outcome of the J.P. movement in Bihar and other parts of north India during mid 70's is a typical example of this inspiration.

A third inspiration is the Marxist and Neo-Marxist perspective. Several persons inspired by this perspective left political parties for a variety of reasons to set up voluntary organisations and gave them an initial meaning from this ideological stand-point. Some people who were involved in ultra-left movements, like the Naxalite struggle, after some time changed their course and also set-up voluntary organisations. Within the Church, the Marxist perspective among some clergy and a debate on liberation theology also inspired several voluntary development organisations in the country.

Historically, the Church has been a major source of inspiration and the teachings of Jesus Christ have been used to inspire whole generations of missionaries to serve the poor and the needy. Christ told, "Verily I say unto you inasmuch as you have done it to one of the least of these my brotheren you have done it to me". (Mathew - 25:40) Among the contemporary configuration of voluntary organisations, a large number of people and institutions continue to receive inspiration from Christian thought.

Likewise, the influence of Islamic, Buddhist and other traditions has also been quite visible.

One of the interesting inspirations of this type is reflected in the Rama Krishna Mission and its various development initiatives throughout the country.

In several parts of the country, inspiration for the founder(s) of voluntary organisations came from social thinkers and reformers like Dr. Ambedkar to work for the dalits and the down-trodden.

9.2 Rationale

The second parameter could be called the rationale for initiating voluntary action. It is almost like a world-view or an underlying assumption of why a voluntary initiative is needed. It is almost like a statement of belief from the founder(s) about what needs to be done in the society for an appropriate change to occur. If we examine the range of voluntary organisations in the country today, eight distinct types emerge under this parameter as discussed earlier.

The first four types are based on the rationale that people need help. The poor, down-trodden and weak need material resources, assistance of knowledge, ideas and skills; The fact that they are poor is because they are denied help. This help or assistance could be temporary, during times of extreme crises or hardship; or this help could be perpetual. Most voluntary organisations operating on a charity and welfare perspective adhere to this rationale. Most organisations providing relief and rehabilitation during events of disaster, droughts, cyclone, floods, earthquake, etc., also operate on this underlying assumption. They tend to treat the members of the community as incapable and resourceless. Their activities include transfer of skills and resources. They also include provision of assistance-based services like mid-day meals, clothing, shelter, medicines, etc.

The fifth type envisages development approach. Here the focus is on people who could do it on their own but with NGO's support, particularly that support in the form of programmes, resources, ideas and skills. It is under this category that we may place programmes of health, education, agriculture, irrigation, forestry, income generation activities, appropriate technology, etc.

The sixth type is based on the theme of empowerment. It assumes that the poor need to get organised and struggle for appropriate change to occur. The focus of intervention, therefore, laid on the conscientisation and organisation of certain sections — poor tribals, dalits, landless, women etc. The ultimate purpose of the strategy is empowerment. The struggle of the poor may be catalised through a variety of activities which may focus on acquisition of assets, wages, implementation of certain progressive legislations, education etc.

And the last two types believe in the need for support and influence at different levels on the struggles by the poor directly and their organisations for influencing policy at the local, district, state, national and international levels. This perspective assumes that with growing internationalisation of our societies and economies, forces of oppression and marginalisation operating from different levels need to be countered and confronted at those levels. Therefore, the support and influence will take different forms at different levels. It is here that institutions engaged in advocacy, research, networking, documentation, training, federating, etc. come into the picture.

These types tend to describe a wide-variety of programmes and activities that voluntary organisations undertake. More than that, they tend to describe the basic underlying world-view or rationale of those programmes and activities. Therefore, we find that a health programme carried out with the first rationale of 'help' tends to provide medicines and treatments, while another one carried out with the rationale of 'development' tends to educate people and solve other non-health related problems in an integrated manner. Therefore, these distinctions are important not merely in their underlying belief but in the outcome as reflected in the manner in which programmes and activities are carried out by such voluntary organisations.

"Further differentiation does occur on the basis of the strategy of intervention. For example, some organisations focus on one sector, like health, education, income generation, forestry, etc. Some organisations are multi-sectoral or integrated in their approach. Some other organisations focus on one constituency say, tribals or landless in a given geographical area. Yet some other organisations focus on multiple constituencies. Thus, it is possible to find different types of voluntary organisations, carrying out the same sectoral work with similar constituencies but having totally different orientation, approach and activities. It is important, therefore, to keep this distinction in mind because this tends to explain the differences that occur among voluntary organisations."

9.3 Size

In our experience, size has become one of the main parameters which explains the difference among voluntary development organisations. Size can be classified in various ways. One dimension of size is the area of coverage. Many organisations are very local, covering few villages. Some are national in their coverage. Related to the question of coverage is the size in terms of full-time and part-time staff and the over-all budgets and resources.

The question of size cuts across the previous two parameters and can be seen as an independent parameter describing the range of voluntary organisations and, the nature of their functioning. It is possible to develop various categories within this parameter of size, but five such categories seem to make more sense.

The first category of small organisations is the most predominant one in the Indian context. These are the organisations which work in a few villages within a block of a district. They have generally many part-timers, volunteers and a few (may be three to five) full-time staff. Most of their funds are based on local resources, some contributed by members of the organisations themselves. They may occasionally receive some funds from outside on an informal or intermittent basis.

The second category of medium size organisations tends to cover a block or two in rural areas. They may have 10 to 25 full-time staff and an on-going project budget based on project grants from national or international sources in the range of rupees 1. lakh to 10. lakhs per year. Their number is also fairly large in a country like India.

The third category of big organisations would be those who employ between 25 to 100 full-time staff at different levels and have project budgets varying from 10 to 50 lakhs rupees per annum. They cover wider area, several districts and they operate on a regular programme basis.

The fourth category could be called large size organisations which are less in number in India today. They would have staff strength of minimum 100 and more and a budget above rupees Rs. 50 lakhs upto Rs. 50 million per annum based on project grants from several sources.

The fifth category could be called mighty organisations. There are few such organisations in the country whose resources exceed Rs. 200 million. Their activities are spread over in many parts of the country. More than 1000 employees chance to work as regular staff including professional experts.

Various dimensions about the nature of voluntary organisations and the issues they experience get determined by this parameter of size and its implications on their functioning.

The above three broad parameters i.e., inspiration, rationale, and size, can be used to classify various voluntary organisations active in India. It is possible to see all types of combinations exist in the country today.

David Carton has beautifully classified the strategies of development oriented NGOs into a three generation family as manifested in the following Table.

STRATEGIES OF DEVELOPMENT ORIENTED VOS
A THREE GENERATION FAMILY

GENERATION

	FIRST	SECOND	THIRD
DEFINING FEATURES	RELIEF & WELFARE	COMMUNITY DEVELOPMENT	SUSTAINABLE SYSTEMS DEVELOPMENT
PROBLEM DEFINITION	SHORTAGE	LOCAL INERTIA	INSTITUTIONAL & POLICY CONSTRAINTS
LIFE FRAME	IMMEDIATE	PROJECT LIFE	INDEFINITE FUTURE
SCOPE	INDIVIDUAL OR FAMILY	NEIGHBORHOOD OR VILLAGE	REGION OR NATION
CHIEF ACTORS	VO	VO + COMMUNITY	ALL PUBLIC AND PRIVATE INSTITUTIONS THAT DEFINE THE SYSTEM
VO ROLE	DOER	MOBILIZER	CATALYST
DEVELOPMENT EDUCATION	STARVING CHILDREN	COMMUNITY SELF HELP	INTERDEPENDENCE SYSTEM-FAILURE
MANAGEMENT ORIENTATION	LOGISTICS MANAGEMENT	PROJECT MANAGEMENT	STRATEGIC MANAGEMENT

DAVID CARTON
U.S.A.

Concluding Remarks

It is believed that more than 30,000 voluntary organizations are actively involved in India with a special focus on rural development. As discussed earlier there are different types of NGOs ranging from charity giving to empowering the people. These NGOs, big or small, have their roots in the grass roots of our Indian society.

5

Concept of Development, Rural Development and Voluntary Action

DEVELOPMENT IN NGOS PERSPECTIVE

1. Development is not a product but it is a process.
2. It is not gathering people but organising the communities.
3. It is not constructing big-big Buildings but Capacity Building among the oppressed.
4. It is not a show piece work but a social action.
5. It is not a mere benefit distribution but People's collective action.
6. It is not giving but empowering.
7. Development is not a piece rate contract.
   It is a strategic endeavour.
8. It cannot be fully achieved with an isolated approach but through a unified, holistic and integrated approach.
9. It is not a mono dimensional act but an a multi dimensional action.
10. It is not an NGO - oriented intervention but people - centred.
11. It is not NGOs itinerary but People's Agenda.
12. It does not deal with inanimate things but with vulnerable human beings who require sensible facilitation.
13. It is not enticing donars but conscientising people.

14. It is not a superficial intervention but a sustainable endeavour.
15. It is not a 9 a.m. to 5 p.m. job but it is a long process that requires commitment, conviction and sacrifice on the part of the community workers.

NGOs working either at the micro or at the macro level are concerned with the development of the unprivileged and underprivileged. The workers of the NGOs hence need to know clearly the concept of development. They are not mere paid jobbers or wage earners in the voluntary sector. They are supposed to be high thinkers though they lead a simple life.

They need to be aware of the purpose they are working for, the objective of their action and the likely impact of their role performances. They need to be sensitive to understand the means and ends in the development process.

Hence NGOs require to understand in depth the concept of development.

Many NGO leaders think that theoretical knowledge does not hold good. Some may blame qualified hands as book worms who are unfit to field work. Of course, bookish knowledge alone will not be beneficial to deal with things in the field. But concepts and theories of development help one sharpen one's thoughts.

Theoretical Understanding Improves one's Knowledge
Practical Experience Improves One's Skill in The Work
In Fact, Both Contribute To One Another And TO One's Professional Efficacy, Versatility and Excellancy.

Hence development workers need to always improve and update their knowledge and skill though for many years they have been practising devleopment work in the field.

This chapter defines the concept of development, the indicators of development, meaning of rural development and strategies for voluntary action.

1. DEFINITIONS OF DEVELOPMENT

(i) Development is referred to a process of continuous progress, unyoking the people from the stages of dependency towards self reliance, assuring equitable distribution of opportunities and resources and ensuring socio-economic justice and harmony among all sections of the society.

(ii) Development is fundamentally a process of transformation that involves the whole society - its economic, social, political and physical structure - as well as the value system and way of life of people.

(iii) Porter (1985) defined development as a complex of three important criteria :

- (a) Economically, sharp and sustained increase in national product.
- (b) Socially, redistribution of national income on an egalitarian basis and incorporation of marginal masses into the money-economy.
- (c) Culturally, emergence of a new social image.

(iv) Development is a process by which a society transforms its institutions in ways that enhance the ability of its people to mobilize and manage resources to produce sustainable and justly distributed benefits consistent with their own aspirations.

2. DIMENSIONS AND INDICATORS OF DEVELOPMENT

The Concept of development can be viewed as a process of realizing certain goals or values, such as improved health, improved housing, better nutrition, more communications, improved transportation, increased command over resources etc. The "more developed" and "less developed" countries can be comparatively studied, and the empirically found differences between them can be adopted to indicate the meaning of development. Such comparisions are generally focussed on variations in per capita incomes, percentage of workers in primary, secondary and tertiary sectors, literacy rate, mortality and fertility rates, etc. Apart from such predominantly economic variables, there are sociological variables like division of labour and social differentiation, rationalization of values and modernization in outlook, and political variables like mobilization and participation, which are associated with socio-economic development of societies.

2.1 Economic Characteristics

Per capita income was first developed as a way of measuring welfare and well-being by Pigou, who described economic welfare as a measurable part of human welfare. Income was also a record of economic activities, of the production of goods and services already achieved. With the identification of developement with national income (GNP) and its other derivatives like per capita income, increase in GNP became the goal of development, and with this the question of promoting individual well-being receded. It was assumed that well-being would follow automatically from economic growth. The resulting emphasis on increase in per capita income as the main goal of development assumed that in the process of development income would "trickle down" to various sections of the society. With the increase in national income, particularly per capita income becoming the main criteria of development, the main effort in developmental activities turned from measures to raise the welfare of the entire population, to measures for increasing national and per capita incomes, believing that this would enable each individual to consume more. This made increase in national income, the predominant concern of developmental activities, and development was understood as a process by which economy was transformed from one whose rate of growth of per capita income was small or negative, to one in which a significant self-sutained increase of per capita income was a permanent long run feature (Adelman, Irma, 1961:Easterlin, Richard, A., 1968).

(i) Structural Transformation

It was recognized quite early that increase in per capita income led to structural transformation of the economy and society. With economic development and increased per capita income, the share of the manufacturing and service sectors of the economy expanded, and that of agricultural sector shrunk. As a result, economically underdeveloped societies had a larger proportion of the labour force in the agricultural sector, while economically developed countries had a lower proportion of the work force in the primary (agricultural) sector, and larger proportion of the work force in the secondary (manufacturing) and tertiary (service) sectors. Based on these structural charateristics of the economy, the proportions of the work force in the primary, secondary and tertiary sectors and the relative contributions of these sectors to GNP were adopted as indicators of economic development. The higher the proportion of work force in the secondary and tertiary sectors, and the higher the proportion of these sectors to the GNP, the country was considered more developed. Inversely, the larger the proportion of the work force in the primary sector, and the larger in share in the GNP, the economy was considered less developed (Kuznets, Simon, 1959, 1965).

(ii) Urbanization

The shift in industrial structure away from agriculture to industries implied the associated process of urbanization, dense human settlements with large proportion of population in nonagricultural pursuits. In developed countries, the proportion of population living in urban areas were more, while in underdevelopea countries a greater proportion of the people lived in rural area. Therefore, the proportion of urban population became another indicator of development (Kuznets, Simon, 1959).

(iii) Capital Formation

Because of the predominance of manufacturing activities in the developed countries, economic development in the early phase was thought to be synonymous with industrialization. Industrialization required capital for building factories, installing machines, and operating the factories for constructing the infrastructure, and various other activities required for the sustenance of manufacturing activities. This led **some scholars to identify capital formation as the main engine of economic development.** Since capital formation is dependent on the rate of savings in the community, it became another indicator for measuring development (Nurkse, Ragnar, 1953).

(iv) Education

Studies by Theodore Schultz (1982) and others on production function indicated that in the creation of increased GNP, the proportion that could be attributed to capital and labour was much smaller than what was expected (only 10-20 per cent) and the residue was the contribution of improvement in human capital. Following their finding, investment in human capital was identified to be an important source of economic development. This led to the identification of the educational level of the population as another indicator of development. Even at this point, the emphasis on human resource development was not as an end in itself, but as a means of achieving higher GNP and per capital production, which continued to be the main objective of development (Schultz, 1982: Harbison and Myers, 1964). But in it the economic dimension merged with the welfare aspect.

2.2 Welfare Characteristics

(i) Social Indicators

Since the Second World War, there has been also concern with the social and welfare aspect of development. United Nations Economic and Social Council has been conducting regular surveys of world social situation, particularly the social dimension of development, such as the conditions of health, nutrition, education, housing, employment, personal income etc., Realising the importance of social dimension of development, an International Committee recommended the following items to constitute the indicators of development: Health including demographic conditions, Food and Nutrition, Education including literacy and skills, condition of work, Employment situation, Aggregate consumption and savings, Transportation, Housing including house hold facilities, Clothing, Recreation and entertainment, Social security, Human freedoms (UNRISD, 1972).

(ii) Basic Necessities

Experience with the social consequences of planned development in Third World countries led to rethinking of the objectives of development. Early in the Sixties Dudley Seers emphasized that development was basically a normative concept synonymous with improvement, and its objective was creating appropriate conditions for the realization of the full potential of human personality. He, therefore, stressed that development was to be understood and measured in terms of the satisfaction of certain basic needs, viz., reduction in poverty, unemployment and inequality, and not through growth in GNP or per capita income. GNP can grow rapidly without any improvement in any of these criteria. The most important requirement for the realization of the potential of human personality was the satisfaction of the food requirement. Below certain levels of nutrition, a man lacked not merely bodily energy and good health, but even interests other than food. He could not rise significantly above an animal existence. There were other basic necessities like clothing and shelter without which personality could not develop. To be chronically dependent upon another person even for food was incompatible with self-respect for a non-senile adult, especially for somebody who is preparing for an economically active life (Seers, Dudley, 1972).

Realization of human potential also requires adequate educational levels, especially literacy. As under-nourishment and unemployment and inequality dwindle, the educational and political aims become increasingly important objectives of development (Seers, 1972).

(iii) Physical Quality of life Index (PQLI)

Another approach to development, emphasizing the welfare dimension, was put forward by Morris D.Morris through his concept of Physical Quality of Life Index (PQLI) (Morris, 1979). He pointed out that even in monetized economy, GNP is not a measure of welfare. The growth of GNP may occur over time without improving wellbeing. The very poorest groups of society may not benefit much, or at all, from rising incomes, some groups may even suffer decline in real income. On the other hand, a country can be made better off in terms of social security, social harmony, length of life, mortality rates, etc. without an increase in GNP. GNP is a measure of production, not of welfare. Life expectancy at age one and infant mortality are very good indicators of the results of the total social process, summing up the combined results of social relations, nutritional status, public health and family environment. The rate of literacy indicates the potential for development and the extent to which poor groups can share the possibilities and advantages of development activity. Morris, therefore, adopted life expectancy, infant mortality, and literacy as the three most universal and important components of development and based on them developed a composite indicator of development called the Physical Quality of Life Index (PQLI).

(iv) Human Development Index (HDI)

The United Nations Development Programme formulated another indicator of development, shifting the emphasis to human development (UNDP 1990). From this perspective, development was defined as a process of enlarging people's choice. At all levels of development, three essential components of development were identified, viz. to lead a long and healthy life, acquire knowledge, and have access to resources needed for a decent standard of living. If these essential choices are not available, many other opportunities remain inaccessible. Additional choices, highly valued by many people, range from political, economic and social freedoms to opportunities for being creative and productive, and enjoying personal self-respecrt and guaranteed human rights. Human development has two sides, viz., the formation of human capabilities such as improved health, knowledge and skills, and the use people make of their acquired capabilities for leisure, productive purposes, or being active in cultural, social and political affairs. Income is only one option that people would like to have, though earlier it was identified to be the exclusive concern for development.

The measurement of human development focussed on three essential elements of life, viz. longevity of life, level of knowledge, and level of living. Longevity of life as an indicator of developement is based on three considerations, viz. the intrinsic value of longevity, its value in helping people pursue various goals, and its association with other characteristics, such as good health and nutrition. Longevity also helps in the pursuit of some of life's other most valued goals, as realization of one's plans and ambitions clearly depends on having a reasonable life span to develop the abilities, use the talents, and carry out plans. GDP per capita is the best available indicator, despite some limitations. People do not isolate different aspects of their lives. Instead, they have an overall sense of well-being. Therefore, it was advocated to be desirable to construct a composite Index of Human Development (HDI), integrating the three components of longevity, literacy and income.

Dr. Amartya Sen, the Noble prize winner also emphasises the significance of welfare economics. He advocates investment upon human beings on their health, education, nutrition, capacity - building would bring about desirable development.

(v) Sociological Dimension

Development affects the structure and character of societies in many ways. Transformation in occupational structure and urbanization that occur with economic development are also indicators of sociological transformation in the society. Comparative studies of developed and underdeveloped societies show significant difference in their mortality and fertility rates. While developed societies are characterised by low mortality and fertility rates, undeveloped societies are characterized by high mortality and fertility rates. Developed countries and countries at very low level of development have relatively low rate of population growth. The early stage of development is characterized by steady fall in mortality rate, without a corresponding fall in fertility rate, resulting in rapid growth of population. It is only at an advanced stage of development that fertility declines. This makes decline in fertility rate a particularly sensitive indicator of development.

(vi) Differentiation

As societies develop, they become increasingly complex in social structure. Simple societies are characterized by homogeneity in the characteristics of its members. Most of the population do more or less similar activities. But with development, there is increasing division of labour leading to social differentiation and social stratification. The earlier modes of distribution of goods and services become replaced by market transactions made through the use of money. This makes specialization of roles and increase in market transactions indicators of social development (Parsons, Talcott, 1967, Polanyi Karl, 1957).

(vii) Modernization

Developed and underdeveloped societies are distinct in many aspects of their culture. **Evolution of universalistic values and norms is an important feature of developed societies.** This is reflected in the institutionalization of a general legal system, applicable to all the sectors of the society, rather few functional or segmental sectors (Parsons, Talcott, 1967). As societies developed, the personality of their members undergo fundamental transformation. They reject passivity, resignation and fatalism and develop instrumental kinds of attitudes and behaviour. The weakening of traditional social organization and culture may create social and personality disorganizations and their expression in various kinds of social tensions and maladies. This makes the political problem of coordination and integration very critical activities in modern societies (Inkles, Alex, 1974).

2.3 POLITICAL INDICATORS

(i) Integration

Though there is some ambiguity among scholars whether economic development is associated with any particular pattern of political development, some believe that in the long run one can see such a relation. Since underdeveloped societies are characterized by the predominance of various particularistic attributes keeping people into disparate groups, the ability of political leaders to integrate such disparate groups into a cohesive community by instilling in them the spirit of nationalism and directing their energies for the realization of national goals is considered a major indicator of political development. This makes nation building, an important dimension of development.

(ii) Political Modernization

Another basic indicator of political development is the establishment of legal institutions, and organisations of political life and the performance of political functions in accordance with the standards expected of a modern national state. This involves the spread of rationality in administration, the strengthening of secular and legal concepts, and the application of specialized knowledge in the solution of human affairs. Related to this is the expectation of certain degree of rational and responsible government behaviour and establishment of political stability.

(iii) Participation

Participation of the deprived sections of the society in the socio-political process has been advocated as an objective of development. Marxist scholars emphasized the incorporation of the marginalized and powerless sections of the society into societal processes as the objective of development. Accordingly, development has been defined as the process by which powerless people everywhere are freed from all forms of dependency - social, cultural and political — so that they can create a personal sense of history for themselves and thereby express their full potential as human beings. From this perspective mobilization of the poor and their participation in socio-political process is the crux of development (Pye, Lucian, 1960, Palmer, Monte, 1980).

To sum up, the foregoing examination of the dimensions and indicators of development indicates that development involves both improvement in human welfare and increase in incomes. While increase in welfare is reflected through indicators such as reduction in mortality, longevity of life, increase in per capita income leads to structural transformation. With it the secondary and tertiary sectors expand and the primary, agricultural sector, shrinks. The expansion of the secondary and tertiary sectors leads to the transfer of population from rural to urban areas leading to urbanization. Development is also accompanied by decline in mortality and fertility rates, social differentiation, development of market, and modernization of beliefs and values. The process of development also leads to integration of societies segmented of ethnic, religious, linguistic and other particularistic basis into a unified community, modernization of political institutions and participation of the marginalized and powerless sections of the society in the socio-political process.

Development is not only a vertical growth but must become equally a horizontal percolation and the same must be enduring. Development is not an interim outbreak or temporary outcome. But it must ensure ceaseless benefits to the community. In other words development must be sustainable.

3. SUSTAINABLE DEVELOPMENT

Sustainable development in simple term means 'balanced and continued development. In other words the concept of sustainable development refers to continuing improvements in the present quality of life at a lower intensity of resource use, thereby leaving behind for future generations an undiminished or even enhanced stock of natural resources and other assets.

Several authors have pointed out that human activities are part of an open dynamic socio-economic subsystem which is embedded in the global ecosphere. The rapid growth of the socio-economic subsystem in modern times has begun to overload some of the capabilities of the ecosystem (locally as well as globally). Many environmentalists argue that unbounded (and especially material-intensive) economic growth would not be sustainable in the long run, given that the ecosphere is finite.

In addition to its environmental roots, the concept of sustainable development which emerged in the 1980s draws on the experience of several decades of development efforts. In the 1950s and 1960s, the focus of economic progress was on growth and increase in output, based mainly on the concepts of economic efficiency. By the early 1970s, the large and growing numbers of poor in the developing world, and the inadequacy of "trickle-down" benefits to these groups, led to greater efforts to directly improve income distribution. The development paradigm shifted towards equitable growth, where social (distributional) objectives were recognized as distinct from and as important as economic efficiency.

3.1 Elements of sustainable development

(i) Sustainability is to live within the regenerative levels of the system.

(ii) It is to bequeath to the future the inheritance received, and therefore to live in the present, without using up the resources of the future.

(iii) Sustainability means the sustainability of the empowerment process and livelihood systems of the marginalized.

(iv) It is the ability of the people to manage their own affairs and prolong the same, till necessary, with their own resources.

(v) It is people centered development by satisfying needs and managing the balance between nature and living beings.

(vi) Dynamic growth, in harmony with nature.

(vii) It is opposed to homogenization.

(viii) It is against the marginalization, or disempowerment, of women.

(ix) Integrated with nature, not to control it.

3.2 Three Approaches to Sustainable Development

It is possible to identify three different concepts of sustainable development that reflect the ideas presented above - i.e., the economic, the ecological and the socio-cultural (Munasinghe and McNealy 1992).

The economic approach to sustainability is based on the Hicks-Lindahl concept of the maximum flow of income that could be generated while at least maintaining the stock of assets (or capital) which yield these benefits (Solow 1986, Maler 1990). There is an underlying concept of optimality and economic efficiency applied to the use of scarce resources. Problems of interpretation arise in identifying the kinds of capital to be maintained (e.g., manufactured, natural, and human capital) and their substitutability, as well as in valuing these assets, particularly ecological resources. The issues of uncertainty, irreversibility and catastrophic collapse pose additional difficulties (Pearce and Turner 1990).

The ecological view of sustainable development focuses on the stability of biological and physical systems. Of particular importance is the viability of subsystems that are critical to the global stability of the overall ecosystem (Perrings 1991). Protection of biological diversity is a key aspect. Furthermore, "natural" systems may be interpreted to include all aspects of the biosphere, including man-made environments like cities. The emphasis is on preserving the resilience and dynamic ability of such systems to adapt to change, rather than conservation of some "ideal" static state.

The socio-cultural concept of sustainability seeks to maintain the stability of social and cultural systems, including the reduction of destructive conflicts (UNEP et. al. 1991). Both intra-generational equity (especially elimination of poverty), and inter-generational equity (involving the rights of future generations) are important aspects of this approach. Preservation of cultural diversity across the globe, and the better use of knowledge concerning sustainable practices embedded in less dominant cultures, should be pursued. Modern society would need to encourage and harness pluralism and grass-roots participation into a more effective decision-making framework for socially sustainable development.

In comparing the concepts of ecological and economic sustainability, Githinji and Perrings (1992) point out that it may be more relevant to examine the maintenance of the set of opportunities, as opposed to the preservation of the value of the asset base. This is because preferences and technology are not held constant through successive generations. So preserving a constant value of the asset base could be redundant. By concentrating on the size of the opportunity set, the importance of the conservation of bio-diversity becomes more evident, both in terms of ecological and economic approaches to sustainability. The preservation of bio-diversity allows the system to retain resilience by protecting it from external shocks, in the same manner that preservation of the capital stock protects assets for future consumption. The difference between the two concepts lies in the consequences of a loss in ecological resilience. Under the Hicksian income measure, a society that consumes its fixed capital without replacement is not sustainable. Using an ecological approach, loss of resilience implies a reduction in the self-organization of the system, but not necessarily a loss in productivity. This depends to a certain extent on the capacity of human societies to adapt and continue functioning in the face of stress and shocks. The linkage between socio-cultural and ecological sustainability is thus demonstrated through the organizational similarities between human societies and ecological systems.

Perrings (1992) points out that sustainable development is not necessarily synonymous with the maintenance of the status quo. Biodiversity conservation does not require the preservation of all species, nor the maintenance of current environmental conditions. An evolutionary system requires that a level of biodiversity be maintained that will guarantee the resilience of the ecosystems on which human consumption and production, and therefore human welfare, depend. Sustainable development demands compensation for the opportunities foregone by future generations, because today's economic activity changes the level or composition of biodiversity in a way that will affect the flow of vital future ecological services, and narrow the options available to unborn generations. This holds true even if positive rates of economic growth indicate an increase in the instrumental (or use) values of options currently available.

Reconciling these various concepts and operationalizing them as a means to achieve sustainable development is a formidable task. The diversity of short-term needs and concerns, as well as long-term goals throughout the world, suggests that there is no universally "right" or "wrong" sustainable development.

One practical approach that may be more useful to policy-makers, developmentalists and the public is the concept of maximization of net benefits of economic and social development, subject to maintaining the services from, and stock of natural resources, especially if they are scarce, should be utilized at rates less than or equal to the natural rate of regeneration. The efficiency with which non-renewable resources are used should be optimized subject to substitutability between these resources and technological progress. Waste should be generated at rates less than or equal to the assimilative capacity of the environment, and efforts should be made to protect intra-and inter-generational equity. Finally, the implementation of sustainable development will require a pluralistic and consultative social framework that, among other things, facilitates the exchange of information between dominant and hitherto disregarded groups in order to identify less material and pollution intensive paths for human progress.

4. RURAL DEVELOPMENT

4.1 Need For Rural Development

In India more than 6 lakhs villages that are complemented with 600 million people constitute nearly two third of the country's population and one tenth of the world. Hence it goes without saying that Rural Development becomes inevitably important.

4.2 Definitions of Rural Development

The Rural Development Sector Policy Paper of the World Bank observed that "Rural development is a strategy designed to improve the economic and social life of a specific group of people" — the rural poor. It involves extending the benefits of development to the poorest among those who seek a livelihood in the rural areas. The group includes small-scale farmers, tenants and the landless". Again a World Bank publication defines rural development as "improving the living standards of the masses of the low-income population residing in rural areas and making the process of rural development self-sustaining".

The World Bank's definition of rural development is based inherently on an operational approach constrained by the practicalitites of allocating loan resources over a wide spectrum of countries, ensuring maximum economic returns to them. In a seminar on approaches to rural development in Asia, discussions were centred around a definition of "rural development as a process which leads to a continuous rise in the capacity of the rural people to control their environment accompanied by a wider distribution of benefits resulting from such control". This definition is composed of three important elements:

(a) Rural development should be viewed as a process of raising the capacity of the rural people to control their environment. Environment does not mean only agriculture or economic development. It includes all aspects of rural life — social, economic, cultural and political.

(b) Rural development as a process should continuously raise the capacity of the rural people to influence their total environment, enabling them to become initiators and controllers of change in their environment rather than being merely the passive objects of external manipulation and control.

(c) Rural development must result in a wider distribution of benefits accruing from technical developments and the participation of weaker sections of the rural population in the process of development.

G. Parthasarathy opines that "The critical element in rural development is improvement of living standards of the poor through opportunities for better utilisation of their physical and human resources"; in the absence of this, utilisation of rural resources has no functional significance. Making the process of rural development self-sustaining not only implies the mobilisation of capital and use of technology for the benefit of the poor but their active involvement in the building up of institutions as well as in functioning of these".

Michael Todaro views that "Rural development encompasses : (1) improvement in level of living, including employment, education, health and nutrition, housing and a variety of social services; (2) decreasing inequality in the distribution of rural incomes and in rural-urban balances in incomes and economic opportunities; and (3) the capacity of the rural sector to sustain and accelerate the pace of these improvement".

Rural development in the ultimate analysis involves the provision of opportunities for the optimum utilisation of the human resources in rural areas. It is, therefore, necessary to base rural developent programmes with the primary aim ofproviding opportunities for the human population to achieve optimum expression of their physical and mental potential.

RURAL DEVELOPMENT PROGRAMMES —AN OVERVIEW

NGOs cannot work in isolation. They need to understand the Governmental interventions in rural development. Massive attempts have been made by the Govt. of India in the uplift of the rural poor. NGOs have to review the past and analyse the present programmes of the Government so that they can extrapolate the future trends according to which they can work out suitable strategies.

HISTORY OF RURAL DEVELOPMENT

There is hardly any parallel in the history of less developed countries in the world over the varied and multi-directional experiments in rural development, by the government as well as voluntary agencies during the twentieth century. Inspite of these varied and multi-directional experiments, in absolute terms, rural poor have multiplied rather than diminished nay eradicated. Rural poverty sticks as a stigma in a way. Rural development has failed but rural development must succeed. So, rural development programmes continue their attack on rural poverty. The government's concern and involvement in this field in fact stemmed from its commitment to planned development. In this process the varied experiments have left a lasting imprint in this vital area of national endeavour.

In the pre-independence days, rural development was primarily a task of voluntary organisations set up by eminent persons with selfless commitment for the rural people. Rabindranath Tagore's scheme of rural reconstruction, the Martandam Experiment by Spencer Hatch, the Gurgaon Experiment by F.L. Brayne, the Rural Reconstruction Programme in Baroda, first initiated by Maharaja Sayaji Rao and later developed by V.T. Krishnmachari, the Firka Development Scheme by T. Prakasam, the Eiawah Pilot Project by Abet Meyer, the Nilakari Experiment by S.K. Dey, etc., are worth mentioning. Mahatma Gandhi initiated different programmes for rural reconstruction as a part of India's independence movement.

The Community Development Programme launched on 2nd October, 1952, and the National Extension Service (1953) were the attempts at rural reconstruction with the aim of associating people, though it became a governmental programme. The area and target group approaches have been made during the planning era in the direction of betterment of the rural people. Implementation of land reforms, different irrigation schemes, co-operatives for credit, marketing and other services, setting up Farmer's Service Societies (FSSs), National Bank for Agriculture and Rural Development (NABARD), the Regional Rural Banks (RRBs), etc., aim at rural development. It so happened that different schemes of the Government have tried to develop one sector or the other without proper co-ordination and integration. In this process, there was only piecemeal rural development and most of the benefits were pocketed by the rich farmers in villages. The rural poor, particularly small and marginal farmers, tenant cultivators, rural artisans and the landless labourers have been bypassed by many developmental schemes.

Despite economic progress in the post-independence period, nine five year plans and heavy investments, the living condition of the rural poor has not improved. Instead, it has deteriorated with inflation and wide spread unemployment. Dissatisfaction with the quality of life and creeping changes in economic strata are contributing to an undercurrent of frustration that is starting to affect basic rural people's attitudes and social harmony.

In the era of planned economic development, the concept of rural development has been defined to mean measures to bring about economic and social change in the rural areas, especially for the benefit of poorer sections. As is natural in a democratic system, the initial attempts at rural development, in this sense, were to set up an administrative infrastructure which would devise and implement developmental programmes and stimulate voluntary community effort for self-betterment.

RURAL DEVELOPMENT PROGRAMMES IN INDIA

1.	Bhoodan Movement	1951
2.	Gramdan Movement	1952
3.	Community Development Programme (CDP)	1952
	National Agricultural Extension Service	1953
4.	Applied Nutrition Programme	1958
5.	Panchayati Raj	1959

6. Intensive Agricultural District Programme (IADF) 1960
7. Hill Area Development Programme (HADP) 1960
8. Tribal Area Development Programme (TADP) 1962
9. Intensive Agricultural Area Programme (IAAP) 1964
10. High-Yielding Variety Programme (HYVP) 1965
11. Intensive Area Development Scheme (IADS) 1965
12. Small Farmers Development Agency (SFDA) 1969
13. Agency for the Development of Marginal Farmers and Agricultural Labourers (MFAL)
14. Drought Prone Area Programme (DPAP) 1970
15. Rural Works Programme (RWP) 1971
16. Crash Scheme for Rural Employment (CSRE) 1971
17. Pilot Intensive Rural Employment Projects (PIREP) 1972
18. Employment Guarantee Scheme (EGS) 1972
19. Minimum Needs Programme (MNP) 1974
20. Twenty-Point Programme
21. Habitat Movement
22. Food for Work Programme (FWP) 1977
23. Antyodya
24. Desert Development Programme (DDP) 1977
25. Operation Barga
26. Command Area Development Programme (CADP) 1978
30. National Rural Employment Programme (NREP) 1980
31. Training of Rural Youth for Self-employment (TRYOEMP) 1980
32. Whole Village Development Programme (WVDP)
33. Special Programmes for Women and Children (SPWC)
34. Programmes for Depressed Areas (PDA)
35. Tribal Development Agency (TDA)
36. National Seeds Programme (NSP)
37. Scheme for Development of Women and Children in Rural Areas (DWCRA)
38. Intensive Pulses Development Programme (IRDP)
39. Summer Moong Production Programme (SMPP)
40. Intensive Cotton Development Programme (ICDP)
41. Village Small Industries Programme (VSI)
42. Khadi and Village Industries Programme
43. Dairy Development Programme
44. Bio-Gas Programme (BGS) 1981
45. Self-employment to Educated Unemployed Youth Programme (SEEUYP) 1983

46. Rural Landless Employment Guarantee Programme (RLEGP) 1983
47. Economic Rehabilitation of the Rural Poor (ERRP)
48. Planning for Development of Villages Programme (PDVP)
49. Integrated Rural Energy Programme (IREP) 1981
50. Western Ghats Development Programme (WGDP)
52. Special Incentive Programme for the Industrially Backward Areas
53. Rural Labour Employment Guarantee Programme (RLEGP)
54. Accelerated Rural Water Supply Programme ((ARWSP)
55. People's Action for Development (India) (PADI)
56. The Social Forestry Programme (SFP)
57. A Tree for Every Child Programme
58. Operation Flood I (OF I)
59. Operation Flood II (OF II)
60. Rural Growth Centres (RGC)
61. Renewable Sources of Energy in Rural Areas (RSERA)
62. Social Inputs in Area Development (SIAD)
*63. Special Foodgrains Production Programme (SFPP) 1986
*64. Special Rice Production Programme (SRPP) 1986
65. Forest Farming for Rural Poor (FFRP) 1986
66. Indira Awaas Yojana (IAY) 1986
67. National Oilseeds Development Programme (NODP)
68. Jawahar Rozgar Yojana (JRY) 1989
69. Panchayat Raj 73rd Amendment 1993
70. Family Credit Plan (FCP) 1993
71. National Watershed Development Project 1996
72. Agricultural Insurance Scheme 1999
73. Swarnajayanti Gram Swarozgar Yojana 1999

ABOUT SWARNAJAYANTI GRAM SWAROZGAR YOJANA

To begin with IRDP was the only self-employment programme. Beginning with Training of Rural Youth for Self Employment (TRYSEM), a number of allied programmes have been added over the years such as Development of Women & Children in Rural Areas (DWCRA), Supply of Improved Toolkits to Rural Artisans (SITRA), and Ganga Kalyan Yojana (GKY). The multiplicity of programmes, being viewed as separate programmes in themselves, resulted in a lack of proper social intermediation, absence of desired linkage among these programmes inter and the implementation being more concerned with achieving individual programme targets rather than focussing on the substantive issue of sustainable income generation. To rectify the situation, Government has decided to restructure the self-employment programmes. A new programme known as "Swarnajayanti Gram Swarozgar Yojana" (SGSY) has been launched from April 1999. This is a holistic programme covering all aspects of self-employment such as organisation of the poor into self-help groups, training, credit, technology, infrastructure and marketing. SGSY is funded by the Centre and the States in the ratio of 75 : 25.

Objective

The objective of SGSY is to bring the assisted poor families (swarozgaris) above the poverty line in three years, by providing them income-generating assets through a mix of bank credit and government subsidy. It would mean ensuring that the family has a monthly net income of atleast Rs. 2000. Subject to availability of funds, the effort will be to cover 30% of the poor families in each block during the next five years.

Salient features of Swarnajayanti Gram Swarozgar Yojana

- Swarnajayanti Gram Swarozgar Yojana aims at establishing a large number of micro-enterprises in the rural areas, building upon the potential of the rural poor. It is rooted in the belief that rural poor in India have competencies and, given the right support can be successful producers of valuable goods/services.
- The assisted families (hence forth known as Swarozgar) may be individuals or groups (Self-Help Groups). Emphasis will be on the group approach.
- The objective under SGSY is to bring every assisted family above the poverty line in three years.
- In establishing the micro-enterprises, the emphasis under SGSY is on the cluster approach. For this, 4-5 key activities will be identified for each block based on the resources, occupational skills of the people and availability of markets. Selection of key activities will be with the approval of the Panchayat Samitis at the block level and the DRDA/ZP at the District level. The major share of SGSY assistance will be in activity clusters.

With the coming into force of SGSY, the earlier programmes IRDP, TRYSEM, DWCRA, SITRA, GKY and MWS are no longer in operation. The unspent balances, as on 1.4.99, under these erstwhile programmes, were pooled under the head SGSY.

S.N	Name of the Scheme	1992-93	1993-94	1994-95	1995-96	1996-97	1997-98
1	Rural Water Supply Programme	460.00	740.00	890.00	1110.00	1110.00	1302.00
2	Rural Sanitation	20.00	30.00	60.00	60.00	60.00	100.00
3	Integrated Rural Development Programme (IRDP)	390.00	654.00	675.00	656.00	656.00	611.00
4	Development of Women and Children in Rural Areas (DWCRA)	13.00	13.00	21.00	65.00	65.00	65.00
5	Training of Rural Youth for Self Employment Programme (TRYSEM)	8.00	13.00	14.00	4.00	14.00	59.00
6	Jawahar Rojgar Yojana (JRY)	2046.00	3306.00	3855.00	3862.00	1865.00	2077.70
7	Employment Assurance Scheme (EAS)	0.00	0.00	1200.00	1570.00	1970.00	1970.00
8	Drought Prone Area Programme (DPAP)	51.26	77.00	85.00	125.00	125.00	115.00
9	Desert Development Programme (DDP)	50.00	75.00	85.00	100.00	100.00	70.00
10	Grants to National Institute of Rural Development (NIRD)	2.00	4.00	4.00	5.00	5.00	5.00
11	Strengthening of State Training Centres	1.50	1.75	3.25	3.25	3.25	3.25
12	Assistance to Council for Advancement of People's Action & Rural Technology (CAPART)	5.00	8.00	12.00	12.00	12.00	12.00
13	Organisation of Training Courses, Seminars and Workshops	0.25	0.50	1.00	0.50	0.50	0.50
14	Strengthening of Extension Training Centre (ETCs)	1.00	1.75	2.25	3.00	3.00	3.00
15	Assistance to Assignees of Ceiling Surplus Land	0.01	0.01	0.01	0.01	0.01	0.01
16	Grants-in-aid to Institute for Agrarian Studies	5.00	8.00	12.00	0.62	0.62	0.68

Table Contd.

Table Contd.

S.N	Name of the Scheme	1992-93	1993-94	1994-95	1995-96	1996-97	1997-98
17	Strengthening of Revenue Machinery and Updating of Land Records	19.99	27.47	27.47	18.80	18.80	18.80
18	Computerisation of Land Records	0.00	0.00	0.00	19.96	19.96	20.00
19	National Commission on Revitalization of Revenue Administration	0.01	0.01	0.01	0.01	0.01	0.01
20	Organisation of Rural Poor	0.01	0.01	0.01	0.01	0.01	0.00
21	Communication Cell	2.25	0.50	2.00	4.00	4.00	4.00
22	Promotion of Voluntary Scheme	5.00	9.50	9.50	10.00	10.00	10.00
23	Organisation of Beneficiaries	1.00	2.50	2.50	3.50	3.50	3.50
24	Panchayat Development & Training	1.00	1.00	5.00	3.00	3.00	3.00
25	Roads in Special Problem Areas	2.00	2.00	2.00	2.00	2.00	2.00
26	Rural Godowns	0.01	0.00	0.00	0.00	0.00	0.00
27	Development of Rural Markets	0.01	0.01	0.01	0.01	0.00	0.00
28	Centre for Agriculture Marketing	4.00	4.00	3.00	1.50	1.50	1.50
29	Establishment Expenditure of Directorate of Marketing & Inspection (DMI)	3.00	6.99	7.99	5.75	5.75	7.25
30	Building for Afro Asian Rural Reconstruction Organisation (AARRO)	0.50	1.00	0.00	0.00	0.00	0.00
31	Rural Housing	10.00	15.00	30.00	45.00	0.00	0.00
	Total	**3100.00**	**5010.00**	**7010.00**	**7700.00**	**6058.00**	**6464.00**

Source : Annual Report 1996-97, Ministry of Rural Areas and Employment.

PLAN POLICIES ON RURAL DEVELOPMENT

Five - Year Plan **1**	**Pollitical Setting** **2**	**Policies on Rural Development** **3**
First Five _ Year Plan (1951 - 56)	Congress Party won the election in 1952 under the towering personality of Jawaharlal Nehru : Period of political stability.	Community development as the method and National Extension Service as the agency.
Second Five - Year Plan (1956 - 61)	Continuance of the Congress Party in power at the centre and in the states (with a few exceptions). Nehru's dominance continued.	Cooperative farming; later, local participation.
Third Five - Year Plan (1961 - 66)	India received a serious jolt as a result of the Chinese War (1962). Nehru's stature declined, in 1964 he passed away. Corruption in high places confirmed by Santhanam Committee Report (1964), and S.R.Das Report against Pratap Singh Kairon (1966). The Indo-Pak conflict took place in 1965. Lal Bahadur Shastri, was succeeded by Indira Gandhi, an uncertain political figure at the time.	Panchayat raj, three-tier model of democratic decentralisation.
The adverse economic situation in the country occasioned largely by the severe drought of 1966 and 1967 made the government declare a 'Plan Holiday', and in the place of the five-year plan, India had three annual plans for 1966 - 67, 1967 -'68 and 1968 - 69. Also, the sixties witnessed the Green Revolution consequent to the introduction of new chemical fertilisers and high-yielding seed varieties. Rural violence also emerged in many parts of India.		
Fourth Five - Year Plan (1969 - 74)	A period of political heterogenelty and fluidity for India. The Congress came into power at the centre with a much reduced majority, but lost in many states where coalition governments of various patterns came into power. In 1969 the Congress was split into the Congress (I) and the Congress (O). The fourteen leading banks were nationalised, initiating an era of populism in politics. The 1971 election was fought and won by the Congress (I) on the plank of 'Garibi Hatao' (removal of poverty).	Special clientele - based and area - based programmes
Fifth Five _ Year Plan (1974 - 79)	Populism continued. A politicallly polarised nation. In 1975, internal emergency imposed, drastically curtailing political and individual rights of the people. In 1977, the Congress Party was defeated, and the Janata Party came to power. The Janata Government terminated the Fifth - Year Plan two years early and drafted its own Sixth Five-Year Plan (1978 - 83).	Introduced the concept of 'basic minimum' needs.

Sixth Five - Year Plan (1980 - 85)	The Congress Party returned to power with a massive majority. It abrogated the Janata Government's Sixth Five-Year Plan and introduced its own Sixth Five -Year Plan (1980 - 85).	Emphasis on strengthening the socio-economic infrastructure in rural areas, alleviating rural poverty and reducing regional disparities. Integrated Rural Development Programme (IRDP).
Seventh Five - Year Plan (1985 - 90)	Indira Gandhi's assassination in 1984. Rajiv Gandhi ride rode to power on the 'sympathy wave'. His Government's emphasis was on alleviation of rural poverty through employment generation.	Employment generation in rural areas acquired primary focus. India launched the Rural Landless Employment Programme (RLEP) and the National Rural Employment Programme (NREP).
(1990 - 92)	Political fluidity in the country with short-lived governments of V.P. Singh and Chandrasekar.	
Eighth Five - Year Plan (1992 - 97)	In the last year of his power Rajiv Gandhi launched the JawaharRojgar Yojana. Emphasis on alleviation of rural poverty continued. In the Parliamentary election congress emerged as a single largest party and Sri. P.V. Narasimha Rao became the Prime Minister. From 1996 to 1999 India faced political instabilities and was governed by hung parliaments. United Front came to power with Prime-Ministership of H.D. Deva Gowda. In a short span of six months he was replaced by I.K. Gujral. However, Congress withdrew its support and without completing two years United Front Government failed.	India launched the Jawahar Rojgar Yojana in which are merged both the RLEP and the NREP. 73rd Constitutional Amendment Bill received the consent of the president of India and the Bill became an Act. This amendment provides one-third reservation for women and additional powers for the Panchayat. Family Credit Plan was introduced. Common minimum programme was announced. Though the Government was favourable to farmers and rural sector effective implementation of any programme could not be done.
Nineth Five _ Year Plan (1997 - 2001)	In 1998 India faced yet another Parliamentary election. Bharatya Janatha Party came to power with the support of certain regional parties. A.B. Vajpayee was sworn in Prime Minister. Vajpayee Government also failed after a tenure of 13 months. Followed by withdrawal of support by regional parties, the Government lost vote of confidence in the floor of the house for want of one vote. India faced another Parliamentary election in September 1999. BJP led coaliation (National Democratic Alliance) came to power.	Old programme continued, Emphasis on promotion of Self Help Groups was made. Orders were issued to implement all rural development schemes through women groups to give impetus to SHG movements. However, Government could not effectively carryout any RD programme as the Government was constantly pinched by its allies. Schemes like IRDP, DWCRA etc. were pooled under the head SGSY (Swarnajayanti Gram Swarozgar Yojana).

- The existing infrastructure for the cluster of activities will be reviewed and gaps will be identified. Critical gaps in investments will be made under SGSY subject to a ceiling of 20% (25% in the case of North Eastern States) of the total programmes allocation for each district. This amount will be maintained by the DRDAs as 'SGSY - Infrastructure Fund' which can also be utilised to generate additional funding from other sources.
- SGSY will also focus on Group approach. This would involve organisation of the poor into Self-Help Groups (SHGs) and their capacity building. Efforts would be made to involve women members in each SHG.
- Subsidy under SGSY will be uniform at 30% of the project cost, subject to a maximum of Rs. 7,500/-. In respect of SC/STs, however, these will be 50% and Rs. 10,000/- respectively. For Groups of Swarozgaris (SHGs), the subsidy would be at 50% of the cost of the scheme, subject to a ceiling of Rs. 1.25 lakh. There will be no monetary limit on subsidy for irrigation projects. Subsidy will be back-ended.
- SGSY will be implemented by the DRDAs through the Panchayat Samithis. The process of planning, implementation and monitoring would integrate the banks and other financial institutions, the PRIs, NGOs, as well as technical institutions in the district. DRDAs will be suitably revamped and strengthened.
- Funds under the SGSY will be shared by Central and State Governments in the ratio of 75 : 25.

4.3 Facets of rural development

Rural Development has the following four key facets :

(i) Livelihood & Income Generation.
(ii) Physical & Infrastructure Development.
(iii) Human/Social Development.
(iv) Empowerment.

(i) Livelihood and Income Generation

(a) Land and land based activites i.e. Agriculture Sericulture, Horticulture, Irrigation, Waste Land Development, Watershed Development, Forestry etc.

(b) Animal Husbandry i.e. Dairy, Goatry, Sheep rearing, Poultry,

Duckery, aqua culture etc.

(c) Cottage and Village industries (i.e.) Spinning, Weaving, Embroidery, Mat Weaving, Basket Making, Silk Worm Rearing, Brick Making etc., and other trades by rural artisans.

These three key components are somehow or other interwoven in rural development because these are the life blood of rural sector which determine the day to day livelihood of the village communities and also the humanity as a whole.

(ii) Physical and Infrastructure Development

Physical and infrastructure development relates to things like Drinking Water System, Roads, Transport, Communication Systems and other linkage facilities concerned with rural socio-economic life.

(iii) Human and Social Development

These relate to Primary Education, Adult and Non-formal education, Skill Training, Social Security, Social Welfare, Health, Nutrition, Neighbourhood, Intra and Inter group harmony and cohessiveness and community tranquility etc.

(iv) Empowerment

Rural development remains incomplete, in the absence of people's empowerment. N.G.Os must be very sensitive and keen that their prime motto and their eventual destination is empowering the people.

Empowerment means giving power and authority to rural poor to control their resources and environment and manage things on their own.

In nutshell, Rural Development is nothing but People's Betterment, be it physical, economic, social, cultural, ecological etc., for the people to live in peace, tranquility and harmony, promoted, managed, maintained and sustained by the people themselves with or without external support or interventions.

4.4 People's Development and Area Development

Rural Development has to be viewed in terms of achieving integration among ordinate and inordinate entities, the environment and time. *This means development of Man as entity has to be achieved in such a manner that it does not unduly affect fellow human beings, other beings, environment and all these over time. Viewed in these terms rural development has to be seen in two broad components of (1) peoples development, and (2) area development and also the union between these developments.* The care that needs to be taken is that while development is taking place in these two components, development in one should complement development in the other and vice versa. The two components of rural development - people development and area development - need to be spelt out in greater detail so as to provide for different strategies which voluntary action can adopt vis-a-vis rural development. People's development, can be seen in the form of —

1. Skill Development,
2. Entrepreneurial Development,
3. Attitudinal change,
4. Behavioural change,
5. Intra-group development and harmony, and
6. Inter-group development and harmony.

On the other hand area development will mainly mean

1. Creation of infrastructure for rural socio-economic life.
2. Betterment of existing facilities;
3. Creation of job opportunities;
4. Ensuring utilisation of facilities by all; and
5. Ensuring sustainability in the use of facilities created and resources available.

Tasks - Soft and Hard

To take the tasks under people's development first, one can say that achieving skills and entrepreneurial development of people is easier than introducing attitudinal and behavioural changes in people. In this respect achieving of intra-group and inter-group development and harmony is tall order. **Thus, the task embodying people's development can be termed as (1) "Soft" tasks (easily achievable) and (2) "Hard" tasks (tough to achieve). While skill and entrepreneurial development can be considered as soft task, achieving of attitudinal and behavioural changes, ability to access and control over resources and intra-group and inter-group development and harmony could be considered as a hard task.** Under both soft and hard tasks a further distinction can be made in terms of more soft (skill development), less soft (entrepreneurial development), less hard (attitudinal and behavioural change) and more hard (intra-group and inter-group harmony and development). The more one moves from most "soft task" to the most "hard task" there is a need for involving people in the process of development and change, which is possible only through voluntary action.

The tasks under people's development also have some inherent in-built relationships. *If only the soft tasks are achieved and no effort is made towards tackling the hard tasks the changes which will result through achieving soft tasks will either be superficial in nature or will be even damaging. Hence, there is need to simultaneously work on toward achieving both the soft and the hard tasks. Since the hard tasks may not be achieved by government through its various agencies, there is not only a need for encouraging the development of voluntary organisations to achieve such tasks on a massive scale but also to achieve unity between the tasks which governmental agencies can perform (soft tasks). Most of the voluntary agencies unfortunately are involved in tackling the soft tasks rather than the hard tasks, and a few voluntary agencies concentrating on hard tasks lack encouragement and support not only from the vested interests but also from governmental agencies especially at the lower level.*

While most of the responsibility of achieving the tasks under people's development may be shouldered by voluntary organisations, the tasks under area development can be achieved by the government through its various agencies. Under area development certain tasks can be performed jointly by government and voluntary organisations. Again, if only area development takes place without proper people's development there are more chances of fruits of such development being usurped by some elite groups. Since the resources, both governmental and voluntary, are limited and scarce it will be prudent to invest them wisely by prioritising the tasks involved and also delineating them between government and voluntary organisations. Unfortunately, one notices a number of voluntary agencies doing the job which should be done by governmental agencies, for example, rural health delivery system and the like. Such experiments, though successful, cannot replace the task which government alone can achieve for all the villages. In the process voluntary organisations end up doing the job which should rightfully be done by the government albeit in a limited way (doing only one function), in restrictive space - (at the most a group of villages) and in a narrow sense (in terms of time only doing it for short duration). Such experiments can at best be termed as good embroidery on a worn-out garment.

Reviews of work done by voluntary agencies in the area of rural development in India will show that most voluntary organisations are engaged in providing services in different fields. In fact, it will not be wrong to say that in the process they have almost reduced themselves to mere extended arms of the government as not only are they dependent on government funds but are engaged solely in carrying out governmental programmes and that too strictly according to the rules, regulations and procedures laid down by the government or donars. Unfortunately, there are very few voluntary organisations which are engaged in achieving the hard tasks - introducing basic changes in society through the process of building awareness, developing abilities and empowering the people, especially the down-trodden, the weak, the poor and the women in villages. Whether or not voluntary agencies should go along with government in rural development will depend greatly on what tasks they choose to perform. If the tasks are in the form of services and some sort of skill training (soft tasks) it is alright for voluntary agencies to depend on government - both for programmes and funding. If the tasks are if one can describe in one term, "conscientisation", voluntary organisations will have to decide to go alone without expecting any aid from government. By government the term is not to refer to any particular government but more as a system embodying political and bureaucratic forces in any society. Hence in terms of introducing changes in societal order government as an institution suffers from built-in limitations.

"Voluntary agencies, in choosing different nature of tasks for rural development, should also be clear about what type of support or encouragement or even opposition they will be meeting with from various forces in society. If voluntary agencies restrict themselves to performing soft tasks, which is what most voluntary organisations are doing in India - there is every likelihood of their receiving encouragement and even support not only from government, but also from different sections of the society. But as stated earlier such work will only be superficial in nature and the terms of introducing changes in the very order of society will be merely skin deep. The contention here is that voluntary organisations like the State are also playing soft and hence are not willing to undertake those tasks which might meet with opposition and bring them in open confrontation with the vested interests."

4.5 Strategies of Voluntary Action

Voluntary action for rural development will be voluntary and developmental only if voluntary organisations enjoy full autonomy - financial, programmatic and administrative-and use such autonomy in performing the hard task. In some cases, in India, the situation is that voluntary action is dependent on the government making people depend on them. Thus the performance of voluntary organisations is no better than the one of governmental departments.

Paulo Freire's conscientisation, aptly establishes that relationship between education and development literacy cannot be viewed in isolation from its social context. Adult education must go hand in hand with human liberation in the broadest sense; with health-care, land redistribution, popular participation in the process of political empowerment of the oppressed and, in general, with the radical transformation of the social system.

Some voluntary groups unbelieving that the people have problem solving skills go on to supply inputs and benefits. Voluntary action should revolve around the voluntarism on the part of people.

Based on Paulo Freire's "praxis" an attempt was made to recommend strategies for voluntary action in rural development (as shown in the exhibits). The concern is that the voluntary organisations should know how to enter, when to enter, why to enter at what stage to enter, and above all when to withdraw. Unfortunately voluntary organisations enter at levels where they should not, achieve the task which they should not perform, and do not know when to get out.

In the process, voluntary action is held responsible for creating dependency syndrome.

Concluding Remarks

Development is not only a vertical growth but also a horizontal percolation. Rural development means betterment and improvement in the quality of the life of the people engineered by the poor and the marginalised with their active participation and the fullest cooperation. Today's NGO's role — position is not a 'bed of roses'. There are many a great challenge before them. NGOs must courageously take up the hard tasks and build up the capacities of the people to encounter the challenges and control over the resources on their own so that preferred and sustained Rural Development could be brought about.

EXHIBIT I

COMPONENTS OF RURAL DEVELOPMENT

RURAL DEVELOPMENT

People's Development (within the people)	Area Development (in relation to the living environment)

EXHIBIT II

SPECIFIC TASKS OF PEOPLE'S DEVELOPMENT AND AREA DEVELOPMENT

	People's Development	Area Development
Soft tasks	* Skill Development	* Creation of Infra Structural Facilities
	* Entrepreneurial Development	* Betterment of Facilities
	* Attitudinal Change	* Creation of job opportunities
Hard tasks	* Behavioural Change	* Ensuring equitable distribution and Utilisation of facilities
	* Intra-group Development & Harmony	* Ensuring eco balance and Sustainability in the use of resources available and facilities created. (eco balance)
	* Inter-group Development & Harmony	
	* Capacity to access and control resources.	

EXHIBIT III

THE EXTENT OF DEPENDENCE OF VOLUNTARY ORGANISATIONS ON GOVERNMENT

More ←————————————————→ Less

Services	Training	Education	Conscientisation	Empowennent

EXHIBIT IV

LIKELY RESPONSE TO VOLUNTARY ORGANISATIONS' TASKS

Most Soft Tasks <————————————————> Most Hard Tasks

Good Support	Encouragement	Indifference	Non-Co-operation	Active opposition

EXHIBIT V

VOLUNTARY ACTION FOR RURAL DEVELOPMENT

Will to Undertake Hard Tasks (dealing with problems and issues)

|

Strategic facilitation

|

Generating, Developing capacity buliding and Prudently Utilising Resources
(Manpower, Money and Material)

|

Turning the Programme over to people and withdrawing

EXHIBIT VI

STRATEGIES FOR VOLUNTARY ACTION

Situation	Strategy
Are the People aware of the problems and Issues? — No	Awake them
Yes ↓ Are they aware of its significance? — No	Organise them
Yes ↓ Are they aware of strategies of solving the problem? — No	Reawake the capacities to analyse causes and consequences
Yes ↓ Are they aware of their capacities? — No	Develop capacities
Yes ↓ Can they solve the problem by using their capacities? — No	Establish logical relationship between the problem and their capacities, strengthen People's organisations and federations and empower them

Yes

THEY DO NOT NEED YOU. GET OUT ⟶

6

Specialities of NGOs' Interventions in Rural Development

People are their subject matter
People's development is their objective
People's involvement is their prime concern
People's management is their destination

It is apparent in the country that the outcome and impact of Voluntary Organisations is tremendous upon rural communities. Their programmes vary from giving immediate relief upto playing the role of advocacy and lobbying. **What the Government could not do and what corporate sector did not do have been achieved by voluntary organisations.** They may differ in their ideologies, be it Gandhian, Christian, Ramakrishna's, Leftist's, J.P's, Frieray's, Professionalist's, etc. But uniformly in all contexts NGOs keep **"People"** as their primary concern.

This chapter highlights certain specialities of NGOs in the process of their development interventions with rural communities. (Of course there are limitations and weaknesses as described in Chapter - 10).

1. REACHING THE UNREACHED

The prime speciality of NGO is that they search out the needy and serve the poor. They go to the people and live with them. They work for and with the unprivileged and underprivileged. NGOs interact with the people at the convenience of the latter unmindful of personal sufferings, unlike Government authorities.

In a Government system we come across the Grievance Days. But there are many people in rural areas who are still unaware of such Grievance Days and even if they know they are unable to reach the Headquarters foregoing their one day labour or due to their crying priorities to ensure their bread or due to lack of transportation or they may lack hopes on grievance days.

But NGOs are physically nearer, mentally closer and socially accessible to the people. Hence they are able to identify their felt needs and focussed needs.

2. BUILDING HOPES

The rural communities are prone to drought and sometimes floods. They lack purchasing and bargaining power. They may attribute their poverty to their fate and destiny. As they had been chronically powerless and suppressed they justify their living condition as an outcome of their ancestral deeds or sins of their previous births and not out of the manipulations of the power structure.

When NGOs first reach villages, perhaps people may be cold and indifferent. Some may suspect, some may be critical, some may be negative, and some others may receive them. From their expressions or gestures NGOs could perceive that the people are frustrated with many things as they live in backwardness and amidst poverty. Of course, in many villages they are deprived of basic facilities like health, education, transportation, electricity etc. In certain cases they do not chance to have potable drinking water within the village and the women have to carry their pots for a long distance. They seem to have lost hopes in life. But NGOs motivate the people to realise that their development lies in their own hands. NGOs' committed approach and devoted interactions with the people slowly build hopes upon the communities. Hope Building is a wonderful process in the NGO's work. This is well experienced by the development workers who involve directly in the development process.

NGO workers are not just going to the people and returning to their hometowns but they live with the people physically, mentally and socially. They dialogue with the members, discuss with groups and convene village meetings to draw their participation. The exposure trips arranged by

NGOs, the social education, training programmes and the community organisational activities carried out by them do slowly and surely build hopes among the communities. The process of building hopes enhances People's Preparatory Process in development.

3. FACILITATING THE ELEMENT OF PROTEST

By element of protest, I mean, the analytical inner drive or the critical psyche of the people against their deprival, denial, unprivilegedness, oppression, suppression etc. As stated in the previous paragraphs the people remain frustrated and undergo many miseries. They attribute them to fate and destiny. Nevertheless, atleast some people always have an element of protest that these things happened to them as something has gone wrong somewhere. This state of mind is defined as an "internal self awareness". This may be 1 per cent or 2 per cent or 5 per cent or 10 per cent among individuals as the case may be. But these elements are suppressed and pressurised by the external powerful forces and hence the same could not be exposed and channalised. The sense of internal self awareness remains in a stage of hybernation.

NGOs identify "the element of protest" among the people awake them and enable them to articulate the same in the development process. The development workers are in a sense, social psychologists to study and encash these elements of protests. Though NGO workers may not perhaps have obtained a degree in Social Psychology, by practice and experience, they are equipped to read the psyche of the people and facilitate the rural communities.

The truth of the fact is that enabling the people to articulate their internal awareness is the starting point of a development race. If the same is articulated people's development is set at momentum.

4. BUILDING AWARENESS

Awareness building is a significant function of NGOs. **Awareness means sensitising the people about their living situation.** People are enlightened to think what they are, what they ought to be and what they can be. Awareness is created through social education programmes, dramas, street plays, exposure, trainings, village meetings, demonstrations, group discussions, PRA (Participatory Rural Appraisal), information sharing, people to people learning etc.

There are organisations which are out and out specialised only in awareness creation in villages particularly through indigenous methods like street plays which exercise a great influence upon rural minds. Awareness programmes propounded by NGOs have brought about attitudinal changes among the masses.

Awareness includes functional literacy. In the evening hours, the NGO workers placed in the villages conduct literacy classes to men and women. This helps the people write their names and read simple alphabets and do simple arithmetics and more so critically analyse the village problems. The Literacy Mission proposed by the Government of India involves a number of Voluntary Organisations in the country to make the programme more successful.

5. GENDER AWARENESS

In the recent years the issue of gender has become increasingly important among NGOs. Today the roles, responsibilities, qualities and behaviour of men and women are found to be socially constructed and not biologically determined. Women are not biologically inferior or less competent. The problem is only lack of opportunities and not the lack of skill and competency.

In India, particularly in rural areas, people are in suppressed condition owing to poverty, their caste system etc.: Specifically the women undergo the worst sufferings and oppressions. Rural women experience a lot of stresses and strains by their own husbands in particular and due to male domination in general.

Research studies reveal that man, being oppressed by so many external forces, tend to express his domination upon his own wife to satisfy his suppressed ego. Hence women in general lack equality in the society and the magnitude is much worse in the women of the Dalith and oppressed classes.

In certain pockets of Madurai District (e.g. Usilampatti) and Salem District of Tamil Nadu and also in States like Bihar, female infanticide is still found in practice among certain communities, which indicate the magnitude of gender disparities.

Hence NGOs conduct many gender awareness programmes at various levels.

Firstly, Gender awareness is created among the staff members of the NGOs through trainings etc., so that they gain clarity and maturity to deal with gender issues. In the community organisation process gender discrimination is being minimised by actively involving the women folk.

In villages, many associations like Farmers's Clubs, Women's Association, Youth Clubs, etc., are organised and these clubs have their Village Development Association (VDA), as their apex body in which also equal number of women executives are enrolled. In certain cases women hold the presidentship of such VDAs. Many such women have proved their capacities on par with or even more than men. Promotion of women Self Help Groups, Mahila Banks, Women's Associations etc. have created greater awareness on women's equality and women's empowerment.

N.G.Os impart awareness among all sections of the rural communities about the practical gender needs and the strategic gender needs. Specifically N.G.Os enable women to access and control over community resources concerned with them.

CASE STUDY

Women and Farmers' Development Association - WFDA

In Chatrapatti Village of Pudukkottai District, a community organiser of CASA was involved in organising a village Development Association comprising equal number of men and women. The men objected to include women in the Sangam but suggested to organise a separate association for women for they had a general feeling that it would cause disgrace to men if women sat on par with them in a public gathering or meeting. Women as a sign of courtesy, usually stand up on seeing men pass by. When the organiser interrogated, the men told that they could allow the women to behave equally within the house but not in the public. It took six months to motivate them. Finally the WFDA was registered. A community centre was built and the same is used by women for making readymade garments. The then lady Collector of Pudukkottai visited the village and extended all possible assistance to the women. Calf-rearing, a scheme exclusively meant for women was successfully carried out by them. All the families were covered under Jeevandhara well-scheme.

Usually when Government officials or Bank Managers visit the villages the women hesitate to come out and speak to them. If any questions are asked to a woman for clarification in the absence of her husband, she may say —

"I do not know"
"Let him come"

"He only knows"
"How can I decide?"
"What can I do?" etc.,

But in the NGO intervened villages, as an outcome of imparting knowledge, exposure trips to outside, skill training and capacity building etc., women are competent to communicate their views to the officials clearly, crisply and candidly. Many of such women leaders are now able to address the public forums on gender issues. NGOs equip women - folk to take-up community management and community leadership roles.

Women's Associations have been federated by NGOs and now they are able to perform their role of advocacy and lobbying and could influence the Government policies.

NGOs positively interpret the 73rd Amendment of the Indian Constitution to become a reality by giving trainings to women representatives to perform their roles justly and independently.

NGOs bring about gender - sensitisation both in men and women.

6. POLITICAL AWARENESS

Politics means 'science and art of governing a country'. Democracy is determined by masses and it is the duty of the state to fulfil theneeds of the citizens. But the majority of masses are exploited by politicians, bureaucrats and elites. NGOs have made a great deal in imparting political awareness among the rural masses who are enlightened as to why they live in poverty stricken condition and how they are exploited by various elements, particularly the politicians. The NGOs motivate the people, atleast in their service areas, to fight for their rights and privileges. They have educated the people to realise their innate, basic and focussed needs and enabled the people to fulfil the same. People accomplish their needs like drinking water, village roads, bus routes, power supply, primary school, health services, veterinary services, fair price shops, noon meals centre for the children, housing etc. through their Sangams. The community based organisations adopt different strategies like procession, hunger strike, gherro etc., as desired by them. In the whole process NGOs remain only a catalyst and facilitate the people to deal with their issues by themselves.

Thus one part of awareness is that the people are enabled to accomplish their needs. The other part is that the peoples are educated to supervise, monitor and govern the public infrastructures and governmental services.

In fact, many reputed NGOs have minimised the role of the service provider but widened their action on awareness generation. Civic-consciousness has been inculcated. The value and power of the ballot paper is made known to them. They are being oriented to exercise their franchise more meaningfully to secure a favorable political climate. As a result, atleast a handful of MLAs to the State Assemblies have been elected with the support of the people's organisations. People are now alerted on the tantalising political scenario and the inveigling parasites. In the present context the Panchayat Raj has become a great boon for NGOs to guide the populace to govern things concerned with them as seen below. In fact development itself is a political process.

7. FACILITATING PANCHAYAT RAJ

April 24th, 1993 should be written in Golden words in the rural history of free India. It is the day when Panchayat Raj (73rd Constitutional Amendment) Bill received consent of the President of India and the Bill became an Act. This is a bold attempt on the part of the Government to ensure people's democracy. Mahatma Gandhi stated "Villages are the backbone of our economy", and the 73rd amendment had surely paved the way for it.

NGOs play an active role to fulfil the dream of peoples' democracy by making it a reality. Their role is significant in different situations. Before the Panchayat election the NGOs motivate and educate the people to choose the genuine representatives showing social concern towards the people than political interest. As an impact of NGOs' involvement many Panchayat Presidents and other representatives have been chosen as unanimous and consensus candidates. In fact, many Presidents of the village Development Associations, Mahila Mandalis, Co-operatives, federation of Self-help groups etc. have been elected as Panchayat representatives. This reveals the NGO's solemn command over and developmental influence with the communities with whom they are working.

NGOs have motivated many women candidates particularly from the oppressed sections of the society to participate in the Panchayat elections.

So also, after the election NGOs organise trainings and other capacity building programmes to promote the competence of the elected representatives to discharge their duties and functions effectively.

NGOs have now started to facilitate the Panchayat in the preparation of micro plans to be carried out by the Panchayat Raj.

Women's empowerment is one of the prime concerns of the NGOs to be achieved through the new Panchayat Raj system. In this regard, multivarious seminars, workshops and training programmes are organised exclusively for the women. NGOs guide the Panchayat Raj Institutions to keep the gender - focus in all the village development programmes. To make a special mention, NGOs like SEWA in Gujarat, SEARCH in Karnataka and Tamil Nadu, Samakhya in Andhra Pradesh and Jeevan Deep in West Bengal have done pioneering work in building up the Panchayat Raj Institutions.

There is a wider scope for NGOs to prepare the Panchayat Raj as a village - based social institution. Once E.M.S. Namboodiripad said 'Democracy at the Central and State levels but bureaucracy at all lower levels'. But the grassroot democracy could be truly achieved if NGOs working with the rural communities, ardently enlighten the electors and strenuously cultivate a social commitment in the minds of the elected.

8. LIBERATION EDUCATION

NGOs, with radical perspective, educate the people who are caught in a never ending struggle for survival - with unsafe water, too little food, little education, and no voice or power in decision making and sensitise them to get rid of vested interests and systemic forces.

Development and education are first of all about liberating people from all that hold them back from a full human life. Ultimately development and education are to transform the society.

Development, liberation, and transformation are the aspects of the same process. It is not a marginal activity. It is at the core of all creative human beings.

Because the bonds of poverty and oppression make the lives of vast numbers of people increasingly inhuman, it is amongst the poor and oppressed that NGOs carry out liberation education through street plays, dramas, simulation and organising trainings, campaigns, rallies, procession, dharna, etc. so as to liberate the oppressed.

Any human view must focus on those whose well-being is denied by others. Progress cannot be measured only by the increase in the total production of a country, because often a privileged minority take for themselves the fruits of the labour of a hard working majority. Millions of people are the victims of a vicious system of exploitation managed by a small powerful group which controls the economic and political life, not only of their own country but of other countries as well.

This system sets up a process which leads inevitably to the rich getting richer and the poor, poorer.

It creates poverty and underdevelopment, establishes classes with conflicting interests, and destroys human dignity in the process.

Hence many NGOs focus their attention first on the liberation of the victims of an unjust society, a total liberation which is personal and social, economic and political. NGOs work to build a new society with the initiative of the people themselves.

9. CAPACITY BUILDING

The purpose of community organisation/development is to equip the people to do things of their own. Equipping the people means building capacities in them. Hence capacity building is the sine-quanon of NGO's interventions. In fact, all development programmes revolve around the human potentials. NGOs attempt to build capacities of the people based on 'what they know', 'what they have', 'what they are capable of' and 'what they can do'.

NGOs believe in the people that they can determine, manage, restructure and sustain their development as they have in-built capacities in themselves. Perhaps for several reasons of oppressions, their capacities remain thwarted. Hence the learning needs of the people are assessed and accordingly capacity building programmes are designed by NGOs.

The rural people are made to realise that human resources are the primary sources for their development than material resources. To achieve human development, programmes are organised to improve their knowledge, competencies, awareness, vocational skills, marketing skills, managerial skills, etc.

9.1 Training and Exposure

To promote their earning capacities, vocational trainings in tailoring, mat-weaving, coir rope making, weaving, embroidery, printing and dyeing, glove making, masonary, carpentry etc., are imparted to both men and women in the villages. In this regard, NGOs avail the assistance from the Government apart from their own initiatives. Close follow-up is made to link the trainees with credit and marketing facilities. Such programmes bridge the gap between what the people lack and what the people are supposed to perform. Many professional NGOs have their separate training units to promote the capacities of the people.

NGOs arrange wide range of **Exposure and Training** to build capacities of the people. NGOs enable People's Sangams to decide what the programme or project they propose to undertake. People may sort out their priorities based on their knowledge. But in certain innovative ventures they really require an exposure in such similar programmes carried out by other NGOs or Agriculture Universities, Veterinary Centres, Small Scale Industries, related Training Institutions etc.

Exposure benefits a lot in this aspect. **The greatest advantage is that exposure enables peopel-to-people learning process which would be more effective.**

There are a few support NGOs whose exclusive role is to train grass root NGOs, who in turn will promote the capacities of the people.

Training is a vital component in capacity building. The objectives of the training that are promoted by NGOs are to impart knowledge, awareness and skill and enable the people to critically analyse their self and social situations and to eqiup them to find alternatives and remedies. PRA is one of the powerful techniques to examine the current realities by the people themselves and to make them realise the root cause of their problems and issues.

Nowadays participatory training methodologies are being widely used by NGOs to involve people in their development. Trainings on leadership, human resource development, general awareness, gender, women's empowerment, environmental protection, rural health and sanitation, family welfare, herbal medicine, income generation, Sangam management, sustainability of Sangam, etc., are imparted.

Through trainings NGOs prepare people to become fit to take up their development task.

9.2 Participatory Training

Many NGOs are well versed in conducting participatory trainings.

Essentially, participatory training is an educational process. This educational process is based on the assumptions of adult learning. The participatory training approach encourages participants to see themselves as a source of information and knowledge about the real world. When they are encouraged to work with the knowledge they have gained from their own experience, they can develop strategies together to change their existing situation.

Facilitated by NGOs, this educational experience takes place in several ways as described below :

(i) Existing popular knowledge is recognised and valued

Participants already possess some knowledge. In participatory approach, the synthesis of popular knowledge with existing scientific knowledge strengthens the educational experience of the learners.

(ii) New knowledge is built on the existing knowledge

In participatory training, the starting point for creating new knowledge is the existing knowledge that people have, particularly the authentic elements of it. As people begin to appreciate what they already know, they are more open to seek new information. This desire to seek new information and knowledge enhances the learning process.

(iii) Participants learn to exercise control

The participatory training puts emphasis on the active participation of learners in generating their own knowledge. This encourages them to take responsibility for their own learning. It is this active posture which constitutes a powerful impetus for learning and for learners to exercise control over their learning.

(iv) It becomes a collective process

One of the elements of participatory training is the promotion of collective responsibility for seeking new knowledge. As a result, participants learn to get together, collectively seeking and analysing information.

(v) It creates informed options

The very process of collectively analysing a given situation throws up various alternatives. As part of the process of analysis, options are debated on the basis of concrete information. As a result, participants are able to accept or reject options on an informed basis. This creates a sense of empowerment which is based on the confidence that information has been interpreted and understood.

(vi) Actions emerge out of this analysis

The very act of involvement in the process of analysing a given reality creates a sense of ownership of that knowledge and willingness to transform that situation. The participants are then able to take concrete action.

9.3 Benefits of capacity building

(a) It imbues confidence among the people.
(b) It enhances hopes among the people.
(c) It improves knowledge and promotes internal Self Awareness among individuals.
(d) It improves the skill to perform the job that people have undertaken be it, vocational, technical, marketing, managerial etc.
(e) It equips the people to manage development projects or plans by themselves. It enables sustainability of the peoples' associations and their projects.
(f) It helps the people reduce the dependency on N.G.Os or other agencies.
(g) It enhances the people to address their problems and social issues with sustained efforts until they attain their goals.

In short, truly capacity building will replace the role of N.G.Os enhancing people to emerge as controllers or governors of their situations or the programmes or projects etc. If N.G.Os fail to carry out capacity building that will only keep the people depend upon NGOs as unveaned calves with their mother cows. N.G.Os who sincerely attempt to build capacities among the people wind up their roles and hand over the same to them, at an appropriate time.

10. INVOLVING PEOPLE THROUGH PARTICIPATORY RURAL APPRAISAL (PRA)

Of late NGOs are popularly adopting PRA technique in the process of planning, community organisation and development.

Irwing wallance once stated **"unlearn what you have learnt and learn things from the people".**

The first step in rural development work is learning from the people. **Through PRA, a TRI-LEARNING PROCESS (i.e.) from people to people, people to NGOs and NGOs to people takes place.** PRA enables the rural people to actively participate in the development process. It gives wider scope and equal opportunity to all including the so called last and the least. In other words PRA is the most useful technique to facilitate participation of all the sections of the people and strengthen the process of community organisation and development.

Participatory Rural Appraisal is a technique which allows one to get information on certain subtle issues. It goes beyond standard answers and tries to understand the patterns and trends as they exist in rural areas. The process of PRA is flexible and prone to modification. As one proceeds to get relevant information from the people, PRA sets parameters for the analysis in the latter stages. It involves the process of 'learning - as - you - go'. The use of PRA techniques depends not only on the existing situation but also on the skills of those who conduct it. An added advantage of PRA is that the process of learning from the people takes place in an informal way, giving them a chance to share their feelings. This can be extended as feedback to the implementing organisations. This helps the organisation monitor its activities and draw up people-centered plans, keeping in mind their needs. PRA as a technique has potential to be applied to a number of situations, say, at the time of appraising a project's feasibility and assessing the impact of a particular project.

Hence PRA technique is used in the entire process of community organisation and development (i.e) from planning to evaluation.

11. COMMUNITY ORGANISATION

NGOs are well - versed in the art of community organisation and they have played a magnificent role in the same.

The truth of the fact is that once the community is organised development is half done.

Two major dimensions need to be observed.

1. Why should the communities be organised?
2. How the communities are being organised?

In the human society we observe the prevalence of powerful minority and the powerless majority. Elites are endowed with power and authority, be it money power, executive power, political power, police power, legislative power, judicial power, bargaining power, controlling power etc., while the poor masses struggle to survive. Down-trodden remain powerless, helpless, uncared, denied, oppressed and suppressed and hence they are invariably IGNORED as a consequence of which these powerless masses need to depend more and more upon the powerful.

Due to economic backwardness and socio-political exploitation these masses are looked down as mean subjects. They remain, by and large, scattered, fragmented, and unorganised owing to various socio-cultural impediments and hence they find it difficult to fulfil even the basic and ordinary things that are due to them.

But if these communities are truly organised such ordinary people can really do extra-ordinary things. They solemnly require an external help, guidance and assistance to get them motivated, united and organised. At this juncture the involvement of voluntary organisation becomes more crucial and inevitable.

In the rural situation there are umpteen activities, programmes and issues around which the communities are being organised : (e.g.)

(i) To get their basic needs fulfilled;
(ii) to promote economic development programmes;
(iii) to obtain the government welfare schemes and privileges available for the poor;
(iv) to promote community based disaster - preparedness;
(v) to promote rural sanitation programme;
(vi) to create mass awareness about structural adjustment programmes;
(vii) to impart gender awareness;
(viii) to organise lift irrigation programmes;
(ix) to promote water shed programme in a given region;
(x) to promote people's agricultural farm or collective farming or natural farming;
(xi) to propagate indigenous medicine;
(xii) to protect the environment;
(xiii) to carryout community-based health programmes;
(xiv) to prevent A.I.D.S;
(xv) to promote self-help groups and indigenous banking;
(xvi) to ensure women's empowerment;
(xvii) to eradicate child labour;
(xviii) to protect and promote cottage industries;
(xix) to enhance sustainable animal husbandry;
(xx) to protect the forest;
(xxi) to obtain minimum wages;
(xxii) to protect the interests of the dalits and the socially oppressed;
(xxiii) to protest against construction of dams etc. at the cost of environment and livelihood of the poor masses;
(xxiv) to influence governmental policies through advocacy and lobbying;
(xxv) to fight against poverty and injustice.

The issues and activities behind the community organisation may vary from area to area or region to region or State to State but the general purpose remains the same. Community organisation is to ensure **PEOPLE'S PREPAREDNESS** to fight against injustice, to tackle poverty and to attain their legitimate rights and privileges.

HOW?

While studying "how" the community organisation is being done by the NGOs it appears to be strikingly grand and splendid. *NGOs with their commitment find a place in the hearts of the people in the course of their involvement. It is apparently true that in the beginning stages people may not happily welcome but rather suspect them as strangers or another group of vested interests. But once the objectives of the NGOs are understood by the people a rapport is established.*

NGOs conduct socio-economic survey of each family of the proposed target group. Mostly the staff already working in the organisation are involved along with other investigators, if required. During survey itself they chance to interact with families and know their problems and issues. Now-a-days, NGOs are conducting PRA to involve people in planning, organising and appraisal.

Before implementing any programme, the NGO workers visit the families, sit with them, dialogue with them and thereby their inter-personal relationship is strengthened. Discussions in groups are also held to learn the varied opinions. NGOs are distinctly known for conducting village meetings to draw the views and ideas of the members of the community in a common platform.

The style of conducting village meetings or PRA exercises and the process of facilitating the participation of the members deserves much appreciation. There are occasions when NGOs sit with the people and vice-versa throughout the night to workout their plans, proposals and programmes. People may gather together after 8.00 p.m at night to deal with certain issues and there are many instances to quote that after long discussions decisions and resolutions were drawn at the daybreak.

NGOs, in their enabling process, have to be most of the time passive listeners, curious observers and track them in line and enhance them to come to a consensus. The government executives, when they attend such village meetings get quite impressed and admire how people are so active and involved in the programmes sponsored by the NGOs.

In the process of community organisation, sangams are promoted, be it a village development association, Farmers association, Mahila Mandali (women's association) Self-Help groups, Youth clubs, co-operatives or other kinds of peoples' body. These people's organisations are federated after a given period of time.

Community organisation is being accomplished through awareness, motivation, education, exposure, training, capacity building, conducting village meetings and PRA exercises, facilitation etc.

Theoretically one may tend to think community organisation is a preliminary process and community development then takes place. But in reality community organisation is a long, ceaseless and intertwined process and sails throughout the course of development.

11.1 Promotion of CBOs

Community Organisation comes to action when Community based Organisations start functioning. NGOs promote different kinds of CBOs say, Mahila Mandalies, Farmers Clubs, Youth Associations, Water shed Committees, Health Committees, Diaster Management Committees, Cooperatives, Environmental associations, Tree Grower Associations, Self-Help Groups, Vegetable Cultivators Associations, Water and Sanitation Committees and the like based on issues or programmes concerned. In the Community Organisation NGOs are very much process oriented enabling people to come together and work out the bylaws, modalities of operation etc.

Here, the concept and organisation of Self Help Groups (SHG) has been described as an illustration for understanding. NGOs by organising SHGs, facilitate a 'silent sustainable grass-root revolution' for ameliorating the lives of the rural poor, particularly women.

12. ORGANISING SHGs

Organising Self-Help Groups emerged as a popular activity among the NGOs during 1990s.

The concept of SHG evolved out of women's organisations (Women Sangams). Earlier, NGOs organised the woman Sangams in villages. The total number of members would exceed even 100 depending upon the women population of the villages. The Executive Committee consisted of a minimum of 7 members. Usually the President of the Sangam functioned as a dominant personality and there was not much scope for all the members to interact in the affairs of the Sangam.

The major participation of women was giving a monthly subscription.

Sometimes the Sangams were registered. They would be awaiting some financial help from the State Social Welfare Board, Panchayat Union, Bank etc. There were incidents that Women Sangams were organised and registered only to avail the grant-in-aid programmes from Welfare Boards and after a spell the Sangams got disorganised, disrupted and vanished.

In other words, the Women Sangams were dependent upon or looking for somebody's help from outside. Either there be any appreciations or accusation of the Sangams, the President was held responsible because she was the one who decided or influenced much on decision making.

NGOs who lived with the rural communities and closely observed and examined such women's activities visualised alternative paradigms to substitute the traditional Women Sangams so as to evoke active participation among all the members of the women groups. They identified the women groups as discerning and potential force among the villagers through whom development programmes could be well initiated. The fact that smaller the group, higher the participation was realised by NGOs and hence small groups of similar interests were organised and found effective. Thus the Self-Help Groups were born.

It is very appropriate to state that India and other Asian countries inherited the principles of management etc., from the U.S and European countries whereas the concept of SHGs blossomed in India so also in other neighbouring countries like Bangladesh and the same is inherited in other parts of the world. It is a pride for this country that many experts from NGOs fly to different regions of the world to promulgate the SHG concept. Many NGOs who organised SHGs and promoted indigenous banking were invited to participate in the conference on Micro credit held in Washington.

Through SHGs, women's movement and a silent revolution among women folk is taking place. NGOs according to their competence organise SHGs numbering from 50 even upto 500 groups, in a given region. Big NGOs like MYRADA, ASSEFA etc., and also many other regional NGOs have organised SHGs in large numbers district-wide and also statewide.

SHGs are motivated to function as **Agents of Social Change**. Gender awareness, social education and trainings are imparted to these groups to improve their knowledge and skill and elevate their decision making power. Each group is restricted to 20 members so that effective participation could be ensured.

NGOs organise SHGs with the following Objectives :

1. To inculcate self-help attitude among women folk;
2. to develop collective leadership;
3. to enhance effective women's participation in their development programmes;
4. to promote saving habit and develop an indigenous banking system within the village among the women folk;
5. to federate these SHGs under one umbrella or apex body not only for credit purpose but also to promote women's solidarity and eventually women's empowerment.

While the traditional Women's Associations look up for help from outside, the SHGs help themselves with their savings and resources. Hence helping themselves becomes the prime motto of SHGs.

12.1 Stages of Group Formation

Various experiments of NGOs reveal that there are 4 important stages in the process of promotion of SHGs. The same are discussed below :

(i) Forming Stage

This is the first stage during which the NGOs explain the concept of Self Help Groups. After listening to this concept, women usually say that they are prepared to form a group. They give their names but it is observed that there exists an innate fear and anxiety. Some come forward to give their contribution on the same day and some others after two or three meetings. It takes one week to 3 months time between their first meeting and first lending. The group is trained to maintain their accounts. Each member gets her passbook from the group for her ready reference. The members choose a name to identify their group.

(ii) Storming Stage

In this stage, a lot of queries arise in the minds of the members of the Self Help Groups. The hidden anxiety and fear flare-up. The conflict between the individual interest and group interest happen to flash. The members tend to argue with the Organizers that their savings will have to be distributed to them after a said period of one year or so. When the members are told that Self Help Group is a continuous process, some of them may withdraw their membership claiming their contributions.

In certain group meetings, elderly women may raise a querry like this; "I am getting old. Suppose something happens next year what will be the benefit for me?". So also questions are asked as to what would happen to the savings made by the unmarried girls after they are married to persons outside the village. Some members pose questions to the Organisers of NGOs as follows: *"You are asking us to contribute our money. How much are you contributing for the group on your part? Can't you give a lumpsum amount, say, Rs. 5,000/- or Rs. 10,000/- to start a viable in group leading? Why should we save if your are not contributing anything for us?"*

This is a crucial stage for NGOs that the members are clearly educated that the Self Help Group has been organized not like a chit fund/group which will be wound up after a said period, sharing their savings and profits. The members are appraised that the group's growth is a continuous process which can run not only all through their lives but even by generations if they wish. Any problem will have to be solved only through the decisions of the members themselves and not by the Organizers. In this stage the group members are ensured that everyone is the owner of the group and not a nominee by the NGO or any outsider. The members have their sole authority to decide as to what to make as bye-laws, whom to select as members, how much to contribute, how long to contribute, how much to lend to each individual, how to settle the account if any untoward incident happens to any individual, what welfare activities are to be undertaken for the village, how they can avail credit from banks and facilities from the Government, how to make the credit and lending systems accountable to each member of the group and also to the financing institutions etc. **They are reminded that it is the women's and women-owned groups for helping themselves and not an NGO's Self Help Group.** In fact, NGOs build up competencies to manage and sustain the groups and to maintain their group's accounts and individuals' pass books. Self Help Group members are being enlightened that self help means, helping one's ownself and that is why self help is the best help.

(iii) Norming Stage

In this stage, members chance to internalise the concept of Self Help groups. In the process of discussions in the group meetings, interactions, contributions, savings and lending, **a mutual trust is being built and established among the members.** Once the sense of being together is enjoyed by the group they tend to speak good about the groups to others. Group morale and Group dynamics are found emerging. Collective decision making gains prominence.

(iv) Performing stage

Both the task and the maintenance functions of the group are clearly realised by the members of the group at this stage. Saving, lending and recovery activities go on smoothly with a sense of implied responsibility on the part of the members. They approach the Bankers for further credit assistance. They discuss about their family as well as village problems. Social obligation of the group is found articulated. They widen their hopes and thoughts that the group can surely be a tool for achieving **socio-economic development** through income generation and **empowerment** through collective action. At this stage the group matures to function on its own.

12.2 Why Should They Save and Lend?

The poor people in the villages largely depend upon the money lenders to meet their urgent and immediate credit needs. It is a sad plight in the rural areas that people in low waters resort to borrow loans from the money lenders at a high rate of interest which is usually 120% per annum.

Suppose a person borrows Rs.100 he/she has to pay Rs.10 as interest per month. Hence in a year totally Rs. 120 is paid as interest alone for a principal of Rs.100. Such exorbitant interests are collected by money lenders exploiting the magnitude of the emergencies and urgencies of the poor and unprivileged because the downtrodden are not easily accessible to the regularised banking system to meet the immediate and important pecuniary needs of the women members or their families.

SHGs offer alternative \ better solutions to overcome such problems. The women members save atleast Rs. 20 or more per month depending upon their saving capacities. Hence, in a SHG which consists of about 15 members a minimum Rs. 300 per month is saved and the same is lent among the members from the first month onwards. Similarly, in the second month again they collect another Rs. 300 and hence the savings is enhanced to Rs. 600. Likewise, every month they save additional Rs. 300 and in a year the total saving would be Rs. 3,600 and along with the interest, the savings will accrue to Rs. 4,000 a year. There is an aphorism in English that little drops of water make a mighty ocean and this has been made true among SHGs.

12.3 The advantages of such SHGs

Even a meagre amount, say Rs. 50 or Rs. 100 can be borrowed as loan.

The right and the deserving beneficiary is chanced to avail the loan on priority. Give and take principle is cultivated among the members.

People who are in exigencies like that of sickness are given preference.

Money is readily available right in the village itself. SHGs chance to create linkage with the Banks, Rashtrya Mahila Kosh and the Government for further assistance.

No cumbersome procedures need to be adhered to in granting the loan.

Almost 100% recovery is ensured. Otherwise the defaulters will be put to shame by the other group members.

Above all, they feel that they are the owners of the group, custodian of the funds and beneficiaries of their own resources.

NGOs promote these SHGs not merely as an activity but as a value based social institution in the village. Looking at the vast potentials of the SHGs promoted with the profound commitment of the NGOs, the NABARD has recognised these SHGs though unregistered.

Accordingly, all the rural branches of the Nationalised and commercial Banks have started linkage with the SHGs at the initiative of the District Managers, NABARD.

Hence, suppose a SHG has a resource of Rs. 5000/- the concerned service area bank provides it with an additional credit of atleast two times say a minimum of another Rs.10,000/- at a nominal rate of interest (below 12% per annum).

The group can grant loan to anybody as the members decide. The rate of interest can be fixed by the SHG itself. (usually 24%). The extra interest so collected from members can be pooled into the funds of SHGs. The bankers will not contact the beneficiaries directly but only the group. This saves a lot of time, stationery and documenting procedures that are involved in granting loans to individuals.

There are SHGs endowed with resources of more than Rs. 5 lakhs. Many exemplary socio-economic programmes, have also been carried out by the SHGs. Here a wonderful case study of a SHG sponsored by MYRADA and patronised and financed by the Indian Bank in Dhannapuri district is given below for reference.

CASE STUDY

VOWAL THOTTAM SHGS DID WONDERFUL THINGS TO THEIR VILLAGE

Vowal Thottam is located 1.5 kms from Othakkadai on the Madurai Melur highway in Tamilnadu. This village is inhabited with 500 families hailing from different caste groups and religions. In 1997, Dr. N. Sethuraman founder of Meenakshi Mission Hospital desired to carry out some outreach programmes to the rural poor. He envisioned to promote Vowal Thottam as a model village. He believed that development of human resources particularly women is the crux of development of the country.

Under his guidance, SHGs named "SEMAM" were organized at Vowal Thottam. Semam means "well being". In another sense it means "to keep the reverses for the future use". Mrs. Lakshmi a widow who was committed to help womenfolk mobilised the local women and initiated to the form Semam SHGs. Their activities are not confined to savings and lendings. They have done wonderful things to their village what men could not do over the years. Some of them are listed below.

1. ***Fair Price Shop :*** The people of the village had no fair price shop. They had to walk to Kodikulam 6 kms. away from Vowal Thottam.

The men had been trying to bring a fair price centre for more than a decade but their efforts bore no fruits. Neither were they serious nor consistent in that endeavour or in any other village development activities. But these SHG women had a meeting among themselves privily unknown to men and worked out their plans to get a fair price shop. Suggested by Dr. N. Sethuraman, they wrote a petition to the District Collector. They obtained signatures of all the SHG members during the night. The next day early morning, a group of ten women left to meet the collector at his bungalow as if they went for market purposes. (Had men known, they would not have allowed women to go to the collectorate).

These women under the leadership of Mrs. Lakshmi met the collector at 7.00 am at his residence at Madurai and the latter listened patiently to the women expressing the crying need for the fair price shop in their village. He assured them to do the needful at the earliest. These women dispersed happily. They wen to the sandy and other places to take car of their routine domestic requirements.

Before they returned to their village, the Tahsildar reahed Vowal Thottam in his jeep with the order from the collector and asked the local people to show a building to open the fair price shop. It was a pleasant shock and surprise for the people of Vowal Thattam. The women immediately located a building. The house owner asked for a rent of Rs. 300 per month. The Tahsildar told that the rent has to be borne by the local people and the women readily accepted to meet the same out of their savings. Accordingly, the shop was opened in the presence of Dr. N. Sethuraman, District officials, local leaders etc. The men eulogised that the SHG members have really done a wonderful job for the common weal of the village. When the shop was opened, only 125 families had had the ration cards but now all the 500 families have been issued the family cards. They regularly get the rice, wheat, kerosine, sugar, atta, and all the essential commodities.

2. The SHGs have pressurized the Government and six hand pumps have been erected. They are blessed with adequate and sufficient potable drinking water.
3. A drainage with a cost estimate of Rs. 3 lakhs was constructed under the direct supervision of the SHGs. This has solve the health and sanitation problems in the village.
4. The internal roads with a cost estimate of Rs. 50,000 were repaired.
5. A bus stop for the village was approved by the Transport authorities. Otherwise they had to walk either to Othakadai or Agricultural University gate walking more than 1.5 kms.
6. Every year, the villagers celebrate the temple festival. The men used to mobilize and manage the finance. But now the women take care of the entire financial management of such festivals. The women now sit with all dignity and honour in the Panchayat and Gramsabha meetings. Their voice is being heared from local panchayat to district administration. They also settled cases with the police amicably and locally.
7. Apart from gender friendly environment, it is worthy to mention that a communal harmony is being blossomed. Vowal Thottam was earlier known for some caste conflicts and issues. Now harmonious relationships are being witnessed among caste groups and people of different faiths as an impact of women's get together meeting together, helping together, working together. They are being empowered socially and economically. In Nutshell, Vowal Thottam SHGs left no stones unturned. Their vision is to empower the 20 villages of their cluster in the next five years. Dr. N. Sethuraman offers constant guidance and

facilitation. So for 560 Seman SHGs have been organized in the districts of Madurai, Theni, Dindigul and Sivagangai. All these SHG's are networked under the umbrella of Mahasemam. Around Rs. 40 lakhs has been advanced to these SHGs by Mahasemam. All these things are possible because of the successful experience of SHGs like Vowal Thottam. Mrs. Laksmi now holds the positions like the leader of the local Semam SHG, the leader of the Othakadai cluster and the board member of the Mahasemam. The hope of the women groups is that every village shall prosper like that of Vowal Thottam.

CASE STUDY

DENKANIKOTTAH'S DASHING WASHER WOMEN ISWARYA LAKSHMI MAHALIR SANGAM DENKANIKOTTAH

Few years back, it was a talk of the people at Denkanikottah about a delivery van plying between Hosur and Denkanikottah. One may wonder what is there to talk about a van. Only further inquiries would reveal that it is not the van but its owners and the purpose for which the van was acquired have created a sensation in the surroundings. The proud owner of the delivery van is neither a business man, nor a transport operator but a group of washer women who have come together under the banner of Iswarya Lakshmi Mahalir Sangam (ILMS).

Flash Back

Organised in December 1990 with 23 members, all except two being the washerwomen of Denkanikottah, the Sangam had the patronage and blessings of the NGO - MYRADA right from its inception. Like many other women groups, functioning in this block, ILMS has also encouraged savings from the members. The accumulated savings amounted to Rs. 18,700 with each member having to their credit a sum ranging from Rs. 500 to Rs. 1,400 MYRADA had provided the group a matching grant of Rs. 4,000. These savings fortified by the matching grant have been used for lending to the members. Each member gets a loan of Rs. 200 to Rs. 500 and repays in a short period of 2 to 3 months. A few members have taken loans for more than 10 times in the last two years revealing that the Group savings provide these poor women an easy access to a simple non-institutionalised credit delivery system for meeting their emergent consumption needs. The loan turnover of the Sangam in the first two years was over Rs. 60,000 with a recovery rate of 100 per cent.

Washer Women's Plight

Notwithstanding the small savings, the economic status of these washerwomen remained dismal. The remuneration they got for washing the clothes was meagre and paltry and their average earning had never crossed Rs. 200 to Rs. 300 per month. Besides, they had work only for about two hours a day and they were idling the rest of the day without any remuneration.

Guidance from NGO - Myrada

In one of the group meetings which was attended by the Sector Officer of MYRADA, the plight of the washerwomen had come up for discussion. Every member had expressed their readiness to work more, if provided with a remunerative job. A suggestion came from a group member as to why the factories in Hosur could not be tried to procure contract for washing their uniforms. Although there were some reservations about the chances of getting the orders from Hosur, guided by MYRADA the group took up the cause and succeeded in procuring the washing contract from M/s. Titan Watches Pvt. Limited.

Tackling the Problem of Transportation

Then came the problem of transportation. A delivery van was the only answer to bridge the gap of 30 kms and meet the contractual obligations to the company.

The Indian-Bank Denkanikottah branch readily came forward to assist the group. They sanctioned a loan for purchasing a delivery van and for meeting their working capital requirements. The loan was sanctioned at a concession rate of interest and without insisting for margin and collateral security.

The women group appointed a driver for the van and an accountant for maintaining the accounts relating to van operations and their dealings with the company.

Improved Economic Status

By virtue of this arrangement, the group is able to get regular orders from the company to the tune of Rs. 30,000 Rs. 35,000 every month and each member now gets an additional income of Rs. 700 and above per month.

On seeing the work executed by the group other factories viz. Rackitt and Colman and Microlab have also come forward with their orders.

Community Activities

The strength of unity has not only helped the group for self development of the members but also provided a power base to demand their just needs. For instance, the residents of Washerwomen (rather washermen) colony had to cover a long distance to fetch a pot of drinking water. The problem was discussed in one of the group meetings and it was decided to persuade the BDO to provide a borewell for the street. The group's efforts have now borne fruits solving the problems of water scarcity of the residents.

The group takes active interest in other social activities like conducting marriages for the helpless and uncared persons of the weaker sections.

[*Source* - Publication by Indian Bank on Groups Dynamics and SHGS].

12.4 Major indicators of effective SHGs

Study on SHGs promoted by NGOs reveals that the following are the indicators of effective SHGs.

PARTICIPANTS / SIZE	:	Small groups of 5 - 20 members.
MOTTO	:	Self Help and Mutual Help.
ECONOMIC STATUS	:	SHG Members are usually from poor families having similar interest.
OFFICE BEARERS	:	The term of office bearers should be fixed with a minimum period of one year. Longer terms allow consolidation of power thereby weakening group cohesion.
MEETINGS	:	Group meeting with a frequency of atleast once a fortnight is found to be strong.
SCHEDULE	:	Meetings with a fixed schedule of day and time.

ATTENDANCE	:	Attendance register will be maintained. Average attendance may be over 90%.
RULES	:	Each SHG should frame its own rules governing its conduct, behaviour, management of finance and activities.
SAVINGS	:	Regular savings by each member is an indication of the member's committment to the group and to personal growth and progress.
COMMON FUND	:	If the common fund revolves briskly it indicates that the group is "Active".
DECISION MAKING	:	Collective decision.
LEADERSHIP	:	Collective leadership.
INTEREST ON SAVINGS	:	The group should be free to fix the interest rate on savings and loans.
RECORDS	:	A good SHG maintains the following account books/ records viz., Attendance register, Minutes book, Savings Ledger, Members' Pass Book, Receipt and Payment Vouchers, Cash book, Loan ledger etc.
OVERDUES	:	Normally recovery is 100%. In case of overdues, it should not exceed 5% of outstandings. Penalties are imposed on defaulters.
PATTERNS OF LOANS	:	Need based and priority based. Most of SHGs functioning well begin with tiny loans (Rs. 500) mostly for consumption purpose and slowly graduating to larger loans for productive purposes.

12.5 Some Observations and Suggestions for NGOs in Organizing SHGs

NGOs educate the Self Help Groups, particularly in the area of accounts-keeping that every individual member must be provided with a pass book which is the most essential part of Self Help Group. This ensures the accountability of the groups and the members towards one another. This avoids suspicion and manipulation.

NGOs link the Self Help Groups with the concerned service area Banks so that they can avail credit from the same. Lending of money raised by the members themselves may not suffice for extending credit for viable income generation activities. The Commercial Banks, on observing six months' savings of the Self Help Groups, grant loans double the amount of their savings. Likewise, the bank will give loans again and again double or triple the amount of their savings. Hence in this process SHGs are advised by the NGOs that savings must be continued at all times though enormous resources are being mobilised from other sources.

The groups must be equipped to gain the confidence of the bankers. There are examples that even upto Rs. 5 lakhs have been granted to Self Help Groups by the banks. The NABARD is very much keen to guide the Bankers in this regard. NGOs encourage and motivate the Bankers too to extend credit to SHGS. In fact, they carry the concept of SHGS and instructions of R.B.I and NABARD to the remote Rural Branches of Commercial Banks and convince the Branch Managers to establish rapport with SHGS and assist them financially and professionally.

12.6 Instructions by Reserve Bank of India

(i) SHGs, registered or unregistered, may open Savings Bank Account with banks.

(ii) SHG lending to be part of the bank's mainstream credit operations and may be treated as a business opportunity.

(iii) Lending to SHGs is an additional segment under priority sector advances of banks.

(iv) Lending to SHGs may be included in Service Area Action Plans.

(v) If situation warrants, lending to SHGs may be exempt from Service Area jurisdiction.

(vi) Requirement of security, margin norms relaxed for lendings to SHGs.

(vii) Defaults by a few members of SHGs/their family members to the financing banks should not come in the way of financing SHG per se provided the SHG is not in default.

(viii) Banks may prescribe simple documentation.

12.7 NABARD guidelines for financing SHGs

The criteria laid down for financing SHGs are as below

(i) The group should have been in active existence for atleast a period six months.
(ii) The group should have successfully undertaken savings and credit operations from its own resources.
(iii) Democratic working of the groups wherein all members feel that 'they have a say' should be evident.
(iv) The group is maintaining proper accounts/records.
(v) The banker should be convinced that the group has not come into existence only for the sake of pecuniary benefits in the project and availing benefits thereunder. There should be genuine need to help each other and work together among the members.

12.8 Wider Scope

There is a wider scope for NGOs in the country to organize self-Help Groups and to link credit facilities with Banks.

Rakshtriya Mahila Kosh, a Governmental Organization, is yet another potential resource agency extending financial support to promote self Help Groups through NGOs. The same provisions could be exploited.

There are atleast 30,000 "Working Voluntary Organizations" in the country. Hence it is hoped that there is every possibility that each NGO could organize atleast 5 "sustaining Self Help Groups" every year.

The SGSY lays great emphasis on SHGs that through the latter credit and development interventions need to be executed.

As Banks and resource agencies like Rashtriya Mahila Kosh SIDBI etc. have launched special schemes to promote SHGs, NGOs in the coming years will better utilise such opportunities and can create a milestone in development in general and women development in particular.

Now many States in the country, like A.P. Government are massively promoting SHGs through Government machineries and federate them under MACS.

The Government of Tamil Nadu has proposed to set up Women Banks in all the Districts of the State. The Prime Minister in his Independence day address (2001) declared that SHGs would have been promoted in all the 14 lakh habitations by 2004 and credit worth of Rs. 17000 crores would be lent to SHGs between 2001 and 2004.

12.9 Networking of SHGs

Networking of Self-Help Groups and federating all such groups under one umbrella has been achieved at the cluster level, mandal level, block level and district level. This has created an enormous strength to the women folk. Networking lays a platform where common issues related to women like gender discrimination, low wages when compared with men, dowry, ill treatment by husbands and their male members, sale of illicit liquor in the villages, atrocities against women and also other issues like basic amenities to the village, environment etc., are being dealt with.

The federation represents the women related issues to the district and the state level officers and get their problems solved and needs fulfilled. In fact, they gain control over the resources and programmes concerned with them.

Thus networking has ultimately resulted in empowering the women folk.

12.10 Women's Bank/Mahila Bank

NGOs have facilitated the Self-Help Groups to join together and pool all their resources as a common fund. With this capital the women groups run their indigenous banks in a central place of all those villages. The women out and out manage the banks without the involvement of any male member. Their banks are run on par with other modern banking systems in the maintenance of records but very much accessible to the members. Their banks are more busier during the sandy days (weekly market days) where women members withdraw/deposit money on account of their transactions.

There are many examples and many models in the country for such women banks. Their resources exceed more than Rs. 50 lakhs in certain cases. It would be amazing to observe such women's banking activities that are promoted by thousands of illiterates and neo-literate women.

Constant and consistent motivation of NGOs have helped these women groups to run and own their banks. Credit facilities are made available to the members timely and justly and a total recovery has been ensured enabling smooth functioning of the banks. Micro credit is being undertaken as a major activity. But this should not be misused as a disguised form of money lending.

13. PEOPLE CENTERED AND PROCESS ORIENTED

The moment one thinks of Voluntary Organisation it comes to mind that they are PRO - PEOPLE. Their activities are essentially people centered. NGOs involve people in the entire development process right from planning upto evaluation. People's participation is the major indicator in the NGOs sponsored programmes. Some say that NGOs are behind the people catalysing the development process. Some others say that the people are behind the NGOs and only on people's strength the NGOs proceed the journey of development. In fact, they are both within themselves as partners of development. The relationship between them is humanitarian, professional and philosophical as the situation demands.

In a Governmental system many development activities tend to be PRODUCT ORIENTED OR TARGET ORIENTED while the NGOs carryout their development activities more a process oriented.

For instance, suppose, the Government proposes to construct a community centre in a village. The usual practice is that they may call for tenders and leave the construction with the contractors who builds the same with the poor quality of materials so that the contractor also gets benefited despite greasing many palms. The people happened to keep themselves as aliens thinking that **THAT IS THE GOVERNMENT BUILDING** and hence it is the Government's job. Even if the local people are engaged as labourers they may not be inclined to check up the construction (the cement mortar, the quality of wood, the importance of curing etc.). They get their wages and complete the work.

In other words, the plan was designed by some Government Engineer, the work was carried out by some contractor and the same centre is controlled by some Government Officer.

But, suppose, an NGO proposes a community centre in the village, throughout the entire processes of construction i.e., from location of the site upto completion, the local people are involved. Each family contributes some amount of money to make the doors, windows, etc., apart from their free labour contribution on turn basis. Everyone chances to participate and so consciously or unconsciously inspects the quality of construction. When it is over, the people may feel that it is their building and it is for them to use for any of their purposes. In other words, in the previous case the construction is an activity which is product oriented and in the case of the latter it is process oriented. It does not matter what was achieved but truly matters how it was accomplished.

In the development work, the significance lies not on the end product alone but the means or the entire processes involved in it.

In nutshell, in the former case, the community centre was built by HANDS but in the latter case by HEARTS and facilitating such a process is the unique role of voluntary organisation.

The Government spends enormous funds on housing programmes to provide home for the homeless under various schemes. It is unfortunate and misfortunate that the housing programme is entrusted to contractors unmindful of the beneficiaries who are going to dwell in the same.

While providing hand-pumps to communities, NGOs encourage the people to construct the platform with their own contribution. Such pumps are maintained by the people themselves.

Generally, when the hand-pumps installed by the Government go out of order, people complain the same to the Commissioner of Panchayat Union or even to the Collector. It is observed that the handpumps sometimes remain unrepaired for months together for want of technical staff at the block level.

But the NGOs impart training to the local youth in the care, maintenance and repair of the hand-pumps and they are given a tool-kit to carryout the repair work. It is not an exaggeration that NGOs have given training to the women members too in the villages who themselves effectively attend the hand-pumps in times they go out of order.

We learn four things from such things

1. NGOs facilitate the people to carry out the programmes with their decisive involvement.
2. NGOs enable the people to gain a sense of ownership and belongingness in the programmes or the assets created.
3. NGOs motivate the people not to be dependent on the Government or the others for little things that could be managed by themselves by promoting a system of self-management.
4. NGOs infuse a sense of moral responsibilities to take care of assets and protect the infrastructures that are created and used by them.

14. COMMUNITY BASED PROGRAMMES

NGOs are known for carrying out varied community based programmes. Few case studies and illustrations are cited herewith.

14.1 Community Health

NGOs have done pioneering work in community based health programmes. For many NGOs health is the entry point for their development interventions. Few case studies are incorporated here for reference.

CASE STUDY

COMPREHENSIVE RURAL DEVELOPMENT AND HEALTH PROJECT, RANGABELIA, WEST BENGAL

This project had its beginnings in 1967 in Rangabelia village of Sunderbans area in 24 Parganas district in West Bengal State. The crude death rate has come down from 19 in 1976 to 7.5 per thousand, infant mortality rate from more than 160 to 39 per thousand live births, maternal mortality from 4.3 to 0.5. The prenatal mortality rate decreased from 136/1000 to 19/1000. More than 60% of eligible couples practice family planning. Major changes in the socio-economic status have taken place, including marked improvement in incomes and quality of life of the Scheduled Caste families.

CASE STUDY

MOTHER TERESA PEOPLE'S RURAL HEALTH CENTRE, A.P.

K.P.T. Palem, Kammavaricheruvu, Malakayalanka and Bhavanipuram (near Machilipatnam A.P) are the interior, Coastal and backward villages located at the sea (Bay of Bengal) mouth of Krishna river. They are frequently prone to cyclones and floods. CASA supported these villages for constructing their houses and other income generation programmes.

Basic Health care was a crying need in those villages. Hence the people approached CASA, Machilipatnam to construct a Health Centre for them. The Development Workers of CASA conducted a Health Survey, held discussions in each of those villages and facilitated the people that they themself could promote a Rural Health Centre to meet out their basic health needs instead of depending upon CASA or other organisations. Dr. Vasumitra, the District Medical and Health Officer of Krishna Dt. and other experts visited those villages and offered their moral support.

Followed by Village Level Meetings, a cluster level meeting of the aforesaid villages was conducted to consolidate and articulate peoples' wisdom and options.

Surprisingly, Village elders and women group leaders came out with an idea that they can form a Health Committee with the representation of all the four villages and promote a Health Centre to meet their needs. They worked out a plan that an ANM could be appointed by the Committee who will stay day and night at Bhavanipuram cyclone shelter and take care of the basic Health needs of the villagers. So also the services of qualified doctors would be hired from Government or non-Governmental sources once a week. The Health Centre promoted by the committee was named by them as Mother Teresas People's Rural Health Centre. They raised a contribution of Rs. 1,00,000. Each family of the four villages contributed. Donations from outsiders were also collected. The same amount was deposited at Andhra Bank, Chinnapuram. The Committee appointed an A.N.M. as planned and her salaries are being paid every month out of the interest earned from the Bank Deposit and professional charges.

The Government Health Department appreciated the Peoples' initiative and the RCH Project (Reproductive and Child Health) is being implemented through the Health Centre. The Government sends a team of Doctors and paramedical staff on third Tuesdays of every month to give Polio Drops to the children and attend other patients. Through this Health Centre anti diarrhoea campaigns are conducted in all the villages, the women are given orientation about preparation of ORS, the Men and Women are educated on AIDS prevention and all age groups of the people are being educated on Community Health. Apart from the District Medical and Health Department of Krishna District, Government Hospital, Machilipatnam, the World Vision of India another NGO, Indian Medical Association, are extending professional and material assistance to the Health Centre. Thus the Mother Teresa's People's Rural Health Centre is out and out a Peoples initiative nurtured by professional facilitation of CASA, Machilipatnam.

14.2 Agriculture and allied Programmes

As Rural Society is agriculture Society, NGOs are committed and have contributed a lot for the enhancement of the farming activities and for the prosperity of rural communities. Lift Irrigation, water shed projects and horticulture are some of the notable programmes by NGOs. Hundreds of small and marginal farmers including Dalit Communities have been benefited by such projects. In countries like India farmers run shot of irrigation facilities. It is widely known that agriculture is a gambling of monsoon. It is a routine phenomenon that crops like paddy, wheat etc. that were raised upto harvesting stage summarily failed for want of last watering. Hence NGOs have designed in consultation with the people, various irrigation models without affecting the ground water source and environment.

The following Case Study manifests CASA's intervention with a special emphasis on Lift irrigation programme.

CASE STUDY

THAT FLOODED MAYANUR NOW APPEARS TO BE A PROUD MAYANUR

There has been a remarkable change in the life style and the standard of living of the people as an impact of CASA'S Interventions. The Dhalit-community members who were rendered homeless during 1977 flood are now seen with pride and dignity.
CASA's interventions can be manifested in 4 stages.

1. Relief : Followed by the 1977 flood immediate relief was provided to the Dhalit people in terms of food, materials, etc.

2. Rehabilitation : Nearly 300 flood victims were resettled at elevated places. The community was motivated to pressurize the Government to offer 3 Cents each. Accordingly each benificiary was granted house site and houses were constructed with the assistance of CASA.

3. Community Organisation : Dairy Co-operative Society, Sheep Co-operative Society, Mahila Mandali, Youth Club, Farmers Association etc. were organised.

4. Development : For the socio-economic development of the people, employment programmes like Spinning Unit, Weaving Unit, Match Unit, Dairy Project, Sheep rearing, Lift Irrigation Project, etc., were promoted.

Among various Community Agriculture Schemes, Mayanur Lift Irrigation Programme is one of the spectacular projects which was implemented at Mayanur village in Trichy District to benefit the flood affected Dhalit people.

103 farmers who owned their lands ranging from 0.5 to 1.50 acres

were identified. As decided by those small farmers the community irrigation project was enunciated.

The plight of Mayanur small farmers was that their lands were situated in close proximity to the Cauvery river but deprived of irrigation. A canal called Amaravathy which was supposed to draw water to their lands usually falls dry because those lands are the tail end pockets of the same. Hence the Development Workers of CASA discussed with the community and motivated them to find an alternative to irrigate their lands. After much discussions, the idea of a community irrigation project was evolved. Accordingly a site of 10 cents of land was purchased adjacent to the Cauvery Bank by the people. CASA helped them to dig a community well providing necessary material assistance to a tune of Rs.1.5 lakhs.

To bale out water, 22 H.P. Oil Engines (2 Nos.) were provided to them. The important feature is that all the 103 families contributed their labour in the construction of the community well. Fortunately the yield of water was copious and plenteous. Water was baled out and their lands were irrigated through the existing channels. The well was completed in the year 1982. Despite bountiful water, it took too longer period for the water to reach the end pockets of the project. Misgivings and conflicts arose among those farmers that they could not draw the water in time to their lands. Then again people sat together to find out an alternative solution. In this regard, the pipe-line installation became a sovereign remedy to fulfil the irrigation requirements of all the fields. CASA played a facilitating role by guiding the people to avail the financial assistance from the Bank and the Government. Accordingly, a proposal for Rs.14 lakhs was designed. With the help of the experts in the field or agriculture and credit agencies, the proposal was finalised and submitted to State Bank of India, Uppidamangalam. The Bank sanctioned the loan for the laying of pipe-line. The Tamil Nadu Asbestos Company which was opened just opposite to the Dhalit Colony extended their benevolent hand in the installation of the pipe-line. The same Company supplied certain type of cement pipes with 50 per cent reduction cost. Thus the lift irrigation society could save a major portion in the project. This helped to meet the cost escalation between the project submission and sanction. Out of the total cost of Rs.14 lakhs, a sum of Rs. 4 lakhs was mobilized as subsidy from the Government. Now agricultural operations are being carried out optimally.

A study was conducted on the lift irrigation project in 1997 by a team headed by the author himself. Many interesting facts are found out. They are —

1. 103 members who cultivate 135 acres of land during 1982 are cultivating 165 acres in 1997. This means additional lands were purchased as well as taken on lease from others.
2. Before 1982, around 2,000 bags of paddy were produced on an average of 20 bags per acre but by 97 more than 4,200 bags of paddy are being reaped during the rainy season every year (one bag contains 60 kgs.).
3. In the second season, crops like maize, ragi, soya beans are cultivated.
4. Some farmers are raising sun flower, sugar cane, banana etc. on rotation basis.
5. During the interview, the women enthusiastically expressed that they are no longer suffering for their food. They usually keep around 15 bags for their consumptions and sell the excess in the market.
6. Almost all the agriculture families do now own their milch cattle, goats, poultry etc. which provide additional income for them. These subsidiary occupations cater to the nutritional needs of the families.
7. The land value which was just Rs. 10,000 per acre during 1982 has sharply increased to Rs. 1 lakh.
8. The farmers feel proud of owning such lands located on the banks of Cauvery.
9. Almost all the farmers are raising the dyncha once a year. This crop supplies enormous bio-mass to the lands, apart from fixing Nitrogen in the soil. In other words farmers are well aware of natural farming methods and the significance of organic farming.
10. These families are now sending their children to the schools regularly.

SPREAD EFFECT OF THE COMMUNITY IRRIGATION PROJECT

It is true, not an exaggeration, that the experiences of the community agricultural project of Mayanur has thrown light upon the on looking farming communities as the same was emulated and replicated in 9 other peripheral villages. On seeing the Mayanur Project, the neighbours realised rather envied it as a magnum bonum for the Dalit people of Mayanur. It has induced the nearby communities to organise similar societies even more vigorously than Mayanur and the Governmental subsidies were also availed by them. The following data give a clear picture about the spread effect of Mayanur.

THE IMPACT AND SPREAD EFFECT OF MAYANUR PILOT PROJECT

S.No.	*Name of the village*	*No. of Projects*	*Area Coverage Acres*	*No. of families Benefited*
1.	Mayanur	1	165.00	103
2.	Vallayalkaranputhur	3	185.00	100
3.	Pudukkottai	1	86.00	72
4.	Lakshmipuram	2	300.00	256
5.	Veerarakiyam	4	360.00	310
6.	Karuppur	1	75.00	60
7.	Mangalam	2	145.00	135
8.	Kattalai	2	165.00	145
9.	Vellalapatty	2	135.00	126
		Total	1601.00	1369

Remarks on Food Production :
Paddy - Average yield per Acre - 30 bags
1601 Acres x @ 30 bags - 48030 bags
48030 bags x @ 60 Kgs. per bag - 2881800 Kgs. or 2882 Tons per Year

Thus Mayanur lift Irrigation remains as one of the mile stones among CASA projects and a pioneering model for Dalit's initiatives towards their development.

As an impact of CASA's interventions over 20 years the following socio-ecnomic development is witnessed as indicated here :

(a) 36 new houses were built.
(b) 43 houses were extended with tiled roofing.
(c) 24 houses were extended with local roofing.
(d) 15 families have added a kitchen room to their existing houses.
(e) As far as education and employment is concerned, Mayanur has created one M.B.B.S., one advocate, one M.Com., B.Ed., (Women), one M.A., B.Ed., (Women), two teachers, one balwadi teacher, two health guides, six railway employees, two employees at B.H.E.L., 15-20 men and women are employed in Private Companies like Fenner Mill, L.G. Body Builders (Automobiles) etc. at Karur.
(f) Self-employment opportunities are provided on various activities. Accordingly one person owns a cycle shop, 2 persons own petty shops, one egg stall, one radio service unit etc.
(g) The other assets purchased and created are as follows :
3 families own motor cycles - TVS Suzukies, 4 families maintain

Mopeds and more than 80 families keep their bicycles. It is cheerful to learn that women in more than 100 families purchased gold ornaments, out of the incomes they derived from various economic development programmes.

(h) 12 members purchased additional lands,

(i) 18 members took lands on lease,

(j) During the past 2 years 45 families purchased their milch animals and more than 20 families, Work bullocks; 100 families, goats; 50 families, Two-in-ones and 40 fans.

It is amazing to know that the houses and the streets of the Dalit Colony which remained dark some years ago are now electrified. More than 90 per cent of their houses received their power connections.

The standard of living and the standard of life of the Dalits have remarkably improved. The stigma or the inferior attitude upon them as 'harijans' has vanished. The people of Mayanur now command respect from the adjacent villages too. Hence it is appropriate to quote that "that flood-affected Mayanur is now appearing as a Pride-filled Mayanur".

Water Shed Development is one of the serious concerns for NGOs working in Rural Development. In different parts of our country Micro water shed projects were initiated even during 1980s availing funds from notable agencies like Christian Aid, EZE etc. Within three years of the implementation of such projects the areas were made green, soil erosion was avoided or minimised and the water table visibly rose up. Based on such few successful experiments of NGOs, the Government of India launched a massive water shed development projects under DPAP during the 8th plan. Micro water shed regions were identified in a given area of upto 500 Hectors to preserve and conserve soil and water of that area. Under water shed programme, contour bunding, check dams, gully plugging, vettiver planting. Social Forestry, Fodder Development, Tank desilting, bund raising, Tank Irrigation Management, Horticulture, Silvi-pasture, Cattle Development, Sericulture, Aqua culture etc. are also undertaken in an integrated approach.

In projects like horticulture NGOs developed some models: (1) covering 10 acres of dry lands and providing the farmers with hand pump for watering the plant; (2) Another model of horticulture is drilling deep bore well for irrigating horticulture plants through drip irrigation systems. Such horticulture projects are being taken care of with the active involvement of local women. There are many success stories that families below poverty line were elevated as an impact of horticulture, particularly orchard. A minimum of 120 fruit bearing plants are planted in one acre of fallow or waste lands (which remained non-remunerative to the poor land holders). The yield per annum after the fourth year comes to atleast Rs. 12,000.

Some NGOs have done successful work in promoting sericulture and aquaculture. In States like Uttara Pradesh, Gujarat, Maharashtra, West Bengal, Bihar etc. NGOs' works on environmental preservation, forest protection etc. through people's movement are also tremendous indeed.

14.3 Animal Husbandry

This is yet another prominent area of NGOs' intervention. Some N.G.Os promoted exemplary models in dairy, calf rearing, goat rearing, sheep rearing, poultry, duck rearing etc. NGOs impart trainings to the rural youth so that they can take care of the local livestock. Some NGOs impart training to couples (Husband & wife) on cattle care and maintenance. To cite, the DANIDA has created hundreds of link worker couples in the villages of Pudukottai district in Tamilnadu with the support of local NGOs. Such couples provide all necessary basic veterinary care to cattle and poultry in the villages. The successful experiments of AMUL at Anand and the like, have been replicated by NGOs working in the nook and corner of the country incorporating the local and traditional wisdom.

CASE STUDY

CORRECTIVE MEASURE OF RASAPATTI SANGHAM

Rasapatti is an interior village located in the border of Pudukottai District of Tamil Nadu. CASA works in the village since 1990. Village Sangam and Women Sangam actively participate in the development of the village. At one point of time the farmers proposed a dairy scheme for their village and as first instance, 20 deserving beneficiaries were identified. Efforts were made by the Sangam members to avail loans but the same were futile since the subsidy portion from the Kunnandarkoil Block could not be released to the 20 members. In other words, the Block could not give a quota of IRDP subsidy to Rasapatti beneficiaries.

Facilitated by CASA, the Sangam members approached then the District Collector. He arranged for subsidy from the reserves of the previous financial year to the concerned service area bank, that is, Bank of India, Killukkottai. The loan proposal was referred to the Regional Manager, Bank of India, Madurai.

The Regional Manager was kind enough to send green signal to the branch at Killukottai. He was pleased to state that the beneficiaries identified by the voluntary organization would be genuine ones and hence the programme could be bankable. The subsidy reached Bank of India, Killukkottai. CASA assisted in processing the application in a short span of a week time. All preliminary verifications and interview with the beneficiaries and their family members were conducted right at the village itself. The Branch Manager clarified with the people whether the marketing arrangements had been made with the dairy Co-op. Society and with the Milk Union at Pudukottai. But the farmers explained that the traditional Milk Co-op. Societies in this area remained a tragic failure. They suggested that the milk would be procured by 2 members of the Sangam who have made agreements to supply milk at the Housing Complex of BHEL, Thuvakkudy, which is located 12 kms from Rasapatti. The Branch Manager welcomed their proposal and granted the loans.

Purchase of animals was done at Uppidamangalam sandy on one Wednesday (i.e.) on a non-banking day in the presence of the purchase committee which consisted of the Branch Manager, one veterinarian of the Panchayat Union concerned and the representative from CASA (the author himself).

During the purchase, one animal was rejected due to its low breed, low milk yield and over-age. Its long horns were painted and its skin was oiled (with castor oil) to minimize its inferiority. As the same was rejected, the beneficiary got in touch with the local brokers and brought a fairly good animal. Hence the same was also tagged.

The animals were brought to the village the same night. The payments were made to the sellers the next day (i.e.) on Thursday. In the evening, the Branch Manager alongwith the CASA representative went to the village for inspection. All the animals including the rejected one had reached there while the selected and tagged one in lieu of that was missing. When the Branch Manager interrogated the beneficiary, the latter grew angry and asserted that he left the rejected one at Uppidamangalam itself and brought only the approved one to the village.

The representative of CASA further checked the animal and found that there was no tag in the ear of the animal. The beneficiary replied that the tag had fallen during the transportation of the animal by lorry.

The CASA representative referred to the signs like poor quality, poor breed, poor milk yield, painted horns, oiled skin, over age, etc. to make the beneficiary realize his misdeed. He was asked to bring the fallen tag. He felt guilty to take out the same from his underwear pocket. It was an embarrassing scene to the Bank Manager, CASA representative and Sangam members. The CASA representative suggested the Sangam members that such mistakes should not have happened in a programme like that which was decided by the people themselves. He advised the Sangam to enquire about this and inform their decision to the Branch Manager. It was around 6 o' clock in the evening the leaders announced that the Sangam meeting would be held at 8.00 p.m. CASA Community organisers were also present.

While such mistakes are quite common in schemes like IRDP programme, Rasapatti Sangam dealt with this case in a different manner. The beneficiary was asked to bring the animal. The same was tied up to the pillar of the temple and after prolonged discussions the people decided that appropriate action might be taken upon the miscreant since the loan was released only on the credibility of the Sangam. It was around 11.30 p.m. in the night that the animal was let on auction.

The next day (i.e.) on Friday morning, to the surprise of the Branch Manager, the Sangam repaid the loan amount in respect of that rejected animal to the bank. He eulogised that Rasapatti Sangam is really smart. He was amazed to state that 'if there are Sangams like Rasapatti's desired rural development could be achieved soon'. He assured the Sangam and granted many other loans like sheep loan etc. as per their recommendations.

Hence NGOs can contribute a lot in facilitating people's Sangams towards successful implementation of Government Schemes. Now the role and scope is more and wider to guide people to avail SGSY.

Some N.G.Os have focused specifically on rural cottage industries and enable thousands of families to come up above the poverty line.

15. EMPOWERING

Empowerment is a concept that goes beyond participation. It implies enabling people to understand the reality of their environment, reflect on the factors shaping that environment, and take steps to effect changes to improve the situation. It is a process that encompasses people deciding where they are now, where they want to go, and developing and implementing plans to reach their goals, based on self-reliance and sharing of power. Most importantly, empowerment helps people liberate themselves from mental and physical dependence. It is, in a sense, the ability to stand independently, think progressively, plan and implement changes systematically and accept the outcomes rationally.

Empowerment means giving power and authority to the people. A separate chapter on empowerment has been incorporated in this book.

16. NGOs' NET WORKING

There exists a general comment that NGOs individually do the best but collectively very less. However NGOs' network is an evolution which now shows encouraging and progressive signs at various level. Over the years certain illustrious attempts were made to promote and strengthen NGOs' network (e.g.) AVARD (Association of Voluntary Agencies in Rural Development), VANI (Voluntary Actions Network in India) VHAI (Voluntary Health Association of India) etc., at the National level and TNVHA (Tamil Nadu Voluntary Health Association) FEVORD - K (Federation of Voluntary Organisations for Rural Development in Karnataka) at the State level and many others in the District level. Networks are being organised around issues like environment, women's issues, child labour, health etc.

There are many advantages for the NGOs to have their network.

1. Networking helps NGOs overcome isolation. Most of the Voluntary Organisations work in small, limited, many a time in remote rural areas. They mostly get busy with their work at the grassroot. But the network gives them the knowledge on the wider national and global socio-political context so that they can relate themselves to the macro environment.
2. Networking helps the NGOs think globally and act locally.
3. Networking provides a mighty strength for NGOs which enhances them to influence the public policy in favour of the downtrodden.
4. Networking ensures a protection for NGOs themselves in the situations when the government and other vested interests in the society pose a threat or make an assault on the voluntary organisation.
5. Networks provide opportunities for interaction, exchange of information, dialogue, joint action among those who may be situated in different organisational settings — NGOs, government, academic institutions, trade unions, political parties, women's organisations, etc., Networks also create the possibility of individuals and

organisations working on a similar issue with somewhat different perspectives to come together, share their information, knowledge base, expertise, resources, capacities in order to work together on that specific issue.

17. ADVOCACYING AND INFLUENCING POLICY

Many professional NGOs have now taken up the challenge to play the role of advocacy and to influence policies in favour of the poor. Advocacy has been detailed in Chapter - 8.

Concluding Remarks

The speciality of NGOs is that, they enable the ordinary people to do extra ordinary things.

The dreams of the oppressed and suppressed do become realities because NGOs do **PEOPLIZE** development.

7

People's Participation in Development

PEOPLE'S DEVELOPMENT IS PEOPLE'S BUSINESS
DEVELOPMENT WITHOUT PEOPLE'S PARTICIPATION IS LIKE THAT OF A WHEEL WITHOUT SPOKES
PARTICIPATION PRESUPPOSES BELONGINGNESS AND CULMINATES IN CONTROL AND OWNERSHIP OF THE PEOPLE

This chapter at the first instance, highlights the definition, meaning and concepts of people's participation for the benefit of the NGOs to critically understand the significance of participation. Followed by that the NGOs facilitation towards participation with illustrations, references and case studies have been potrayed. By virtue of being an NGO-person working directly with the people for a score of years, I firmly believe that People's Development is People's Business. The essence of the essence of development is nothing but people's participation. There are many components that are involved in development like money, material resources, technology, human etc. Of all, the social components or the human factors are the crucial elements. In other words people are the pivot around whom the entire development processess are supposed to revolve.

NGOs have done a pioneering work in arousing people's participation in various rural development programmes and issues like community agriculture, lift irrigation scheme, co-operative people's farming, watershed development, horticulture, sericulture, acquaculture, dairy development and other animal husbandry programmes, cottage industries, community health, adult and non-formal literacy, social forestry, joint forest management, indigenous banking, eradication of child labour, minimum wages, land for the tillers, abolition of alchoholism, environmental protection, women's empowerment, net-working, influencing policies through advocacy, lobbying etc.

1. PEOPLES' PARTICIPATION - (IN A NEW ROBE)

Nowadays, NGOs are very much concerned about the concept of PARTICIPATORY DEVELOPMENT and PEOPLE CENTRED DEVELOPMENT. The aforesaid terms authentically accentuate the involvement of people from the process of planning upto appraisal. Development is determined by the people. To highlight the prominence of people's participation the UNDP (United Nations Development Programme) published in 1990, the first Human Development Report. This created a new paradigm of development called human development paradigm. This paradigm emphasises that the real objective of development is to increase people's development choices. The concept of human development is elaborated along the following lines.

People must be at the centre of human development. Development has to be woven around people, not people around development. It has to be development of the people, by the people and for the people, David C. Korten has articulated such concept of people's involvement as people centred development. People are the primary subject matter in people centred development. Earlier, in the growth centred development, production occupied a significant place.

Development is no longer a favour or a privilege to the people. They cannot be treated as mute observers or objects or passive input receivers as they are powerless and unendowed. They are supposed to be the prime movers of development at any given point of time.

There are many actors in development. No stakeholders can stake the claim over people's development, whether or not they provide resources for them. The stakeholders, be it a local NGO or the multinational, can intervene to facilitate the process but are not supposed to hinder the flow of thoughts and community action under their thumb of resources.

2. DEFINITIONS OF PEOPLE'S PARTICIPATION

"It is a process wherein people involve themselves in planning, decision making and carrying out activities, projects, movement or what so ever towards betterment with or without external support and sustain the same as individuals, people's organisations and social institutions."

"The act of taking part or having a share with others in some action." (Parry, 1972)

"A means for a widening and redistribution of opportunities to take part in societal decision making, in contributing to development and in benefiting from its fruits". — (Paper published by International Labour Organisation).

"Participation includes people's involvement in decision making processes, in implementing programmes .... their sharing in the benefits of development programmes and their involvement in the efforts to evaluate such programmes." (N.T. Uphooff and J. Cohen in the paper "Feasibility and Application of Rural Development Participation.)"

"Participation is concerned with the organised efforts to increase control over resources and regulative institutions in a given social situation, on the part of the groups and movements of those hitherto excluded from such control". (A Pearse and Sjjefel in their book "Inquiry into participation").

"A process by which the members of a society increase their personal and institutional capacities to mobilize and manage resources to produce sustainable and justly distributed improvements in their quality of life consistent with their own aspiration". — David C. Korten.

What is Participation

It can be historically traced that participation as a concept and a strategy of development is an outcome of a profound disillusionment with established development strategy in post Industrial Revolution period. Specifically, the experiences of the fifties and the sixties have demonstrated the fundamental weakness of the top-down, GNP-focused, growth centred strategy of development based on professional expertise and modernized technologies. The development strategy followed during this period emphasized economic growth and industrialization in the context of increasingly centralized planning and control over the distribution of resources.

It is widely accepted that the term 'participation' is too dynamic to have a static and universal definition. Further more, participation is shrouded with a variety of interpretations ranging from "manipulative participation" to "authentic participation". Making political capital out of participation is often a hidden agenda behind the former interpretation whereas the latter stresses on genuine people's involvement as an ongoing process and an end in itself. Hence, an effort can be made to highlight the major strands with regard to various conceptualization and interpretations.

3. CONCEPT OF PARTICIPATION

There are, as Peter Oakley, (1991), identifies, two broadly distinguishable schools of thought on conceptualization of participation.

One school views participation in the context of development project as the key input in terms of the inclusion of human resource in development efforts. This enhances the chances of success of the project.

The other school relates to the means and end debate on participation. To elucidate further, participation as a means implies the use of participation as a strategic component to achieve some predetermined goal or objective. In this sense, participation is essentially a short-term exercise, limited to achievement of certain goal.

Participation as an end is an entirely different concept. Here, participation is seen as a process which unfolds over time and whose purpose is to develop and strengthen the capabilities of rural people to intervene more directly in development activities.

V. Jagannathan opines that in development literature the term "involvement" will be more appropriate and more acceptable concept than participation.

While participation broadly implies "sharing" the term involvement on the other hand connotes a sense of responsibleness and belongingness. It also ensures a sense of oneness and own-ness. But in reality participation is also interpreted as involvement.

Through participation, individuals particularly the poor and powerless chance to influence environment. For them, the environment is what they see, feel and experience. The poor visualise their development in concurrence with their needs and requirements. Hence development has to be practical and favourable to the poor. Studies on Green Revolution reveal that the same has brought many tragedies to the poor as they are incorporated in the modern political, economic and technology systems which are terribly unfavourable to them and over which they have no control. Hence participation cannot be seen as a ..... technique but as a reality.

3.1 Common Participation

In our every day life the rural people take part or interact with others on a variety of activities, and situations, casually incidentally purposely, or necessarily, without which society will not function. They may participate individually or collectively in their agricultural operations, craft, other transactions and so on. All these things are usually carried out. Hence such activities may be classified as ***common participation.***

3.2 Two Distinct Participations

Two distinct people's participations scenario emerge; one, community participation facilitating external project designers achieving the goals which the designers have set for the community and two, communities by participation setting their own goals and achieving them. Thus, the academic debate on development participation could relate to two situations viz. participation in development and participatory development. In the former situation, the project objectives are already set and the communities are made to involve through focused education specific to the project and by forming people's organisations to achieve the project objectives, providing incentives and mobilising them mainly by social control exerted through local leaders. And in the latter, the communities become participatory through a process.

"To be effective, participation must be direct and give ultimate control to local communities so that they can themselves decide their own affairs (p. 9)". In Medleys view "... the new concept of community participation involves an aggressive critique of existing power structures and social condition and requires a far more direct role for ordinary people in deciding matters affecting their welfare". Oakley and Marsden (1984:89) have a very similar view: "... the meaningful participation of the rural poor in development and some active involvement and influence in the decisions affecting those resources. To participate meaningfully implies the ability positively to influence the course of events". They argue that NGOs have an important part to play in this process, and that formal bureaucracies tend to resist it. A similar view point is held by Midgley (1986:150). He has argued that "Although spontaneous participation may appear to be highly desirable.." local communities"... require the stimulus of external agents if they are to participate meaningfully ... NGOs are more likely to promote authentic forms of participation than the state". Midgley also points out to the fact that the bureaucracy is more likely to respond to pressures from "organised interest groups" than from communities at large. Moreover, "Since the least organised and marginalised sections of society have little opportunity to influence government, their interests are not likely to be served by state involvement in community participation" and hence "Non-governmental organisations are not only more likely to serve the interests of the poor but also capable of initiating schemes that increase the organisational power and consequently the political pressures that can be exerted by poor people". (These views have been shared by a number of authors; Hall, Hardiman, Padron, Galijart, Hollnsteiner to name a few).

One does not take part with another unless there is a need, an interest to do so - the outcome would also benefit others, and/or individually one would not be able to influence, secure an outcome of decision-making favourably. One may also find that the word 'influencing' is increasingly being used to denote the type of strategic action that is required on the part of the participants irrespective of the context.

The literature increasingly indicates that participation has an aim — an objective. This would imply that the new participants desire a particular outcome and so, along with (like-minded) others they take strategic action to influence decision-making, seen as a process (a series of outcomes), or to influence a community from preventing a desired outcome from happening, for example, caste discriminatory practices enforced by the caste-Hindus.

As leadership is defined as an act of influencing others, taking part by the poor in decision-making would mean, in simple terms, the 'act of influencing with others'.

Thus participation includes also the "organised efforts to increase control over resources".

Participation involves action. Participation involves 'strategic action' in the light of the fact that participation is occasionally extended to include a state of mind of participants. A person is also said to participate when he is actively concerned about something, whether or not he takes action to demonstrate his concern (passive participants). If a person is involved in an activity, his mind is generally also so engaged, but there can be no presumption of action solely because there is concern (Richardson, 1983) and the reverse is also true i.e. there can be no presumption of concern solely because there is action. Nor is action alone participation. This aspect is crucial to understanding the concept of participation.

Uphoff and Cohen (1979) hold that popular participation should be broadly understood as the active involvement of people in the decision-making process in so far as it affects them. Oakley and Marsden (1984:21) find a whole genre of "participation" literature (also, Uphoff and Cohen, 1979; Lisk, 1981) dealing with rural populations' supposed participation in decision-making, implementation, sharing of benefits and evaluation of development action. Proponents of this view, e.g. Uphoff and Cohen, have argued the need for decentralisation, establishment of local level planning mechanisms and co-ordination at local level. In their discussion, the role of participation in decision-making is restricted to the planning process only.

Participation in implementation has often been viewed as the contribution of resources. But the wider practice is that basic decisions (which underlie development action) are taken already and then the rural population is persuaded, mobilised or invited to endorse the actions, or become involved in them. Mobilisation in this sense is for capital formation and to relieve scarce resources. *In this form, participation is conceived as a manageable input, eventually, a passive form* (Oakley and Marsden, 1984:22).

The shift in the participation argument, therefore, is towards empowerment - increased socio-political control - of the less powerful, and that equation is a substantial condition for participation ('empower' literally means 'to give legal or moral power to; to authorise').

Richardson states that the concept of power is crucial for analysing the impact of participation in practice, but its incorporation into a definition of participation does little to aid understanding it.

Richardson defines power as the capability to determine 'outcome'.

3.3 Peter Oakley's Interpretations

(i) Participation as Collaboration

People in the less developed countries, voluntarily or through persuasion agree to collaborate with an externally determined development project. While the people may participate in the project through their collaboration, they do not have any direct involvement in programme, design, control or management. People's collaboration is sought only as a means to ensure success of the programme. *This interpretation of participation dominates much of the practice of development programmes and projects.*

(ii) Participation as specific targetting of project benefeciaries

Participation is seen as ***inclusion of previously excluded groups*** such as small farmers, or the landless by targetting the benefits directly at them. Often emphasis is put on direct involvement of people (beneficiaries) in the direction and execution of development projects.

(iii) Participation as Organisation

It is argued that most people, and particularly rural people are unable to participate in development activities due to lack of an organisation, (co-operatives, farmers associations etc.). They may slowly emerge as a result of the process of participation.

(iv) Participation as empowering

Participation as means of empowering people has gained increasing support. However the term empowerment is seen differently by different people. Some see empowering as development of skills and abilities to enable people to manage better, to have a say or to be negotiable with the existing delivery system, others see it as more fundamentally political and concerned with enabling people to decide upon and to take actions they believe to be essential for their own development.

While above interpretations represent different streams of thoughts and conceptualizations, they should not be treated as separate and discrete categories. Local people's contribution is pre requisite to organisation and empowerment. At the same time organisation which is a fundamental ingredient of the process of empowering, is also a pre requisite to local people's contribution.

It is naive to define participation in rigid terms. Rather it is suggested that participation must always be described in terms of its specific context. This requirement recognises the variety of interpretations and at the same time provides scope for a specific definition within a contextual frame of reference.

The concept of development seems to provide a context for participation. Development is seen as the increasing possibility of the individual to control his own 'environment'. Thus, people's participation appears not merely as an utopian ideal but as a necessity.

4. COMPONENTS OF PARTICIPATION

4.1 Labour Contribution

Labour is a primary component of participation as far as the rural communities are concerned. Schemes like construction of road, community hall, community well, deepening of pond desilting of the inflow channel, land reclamation, social forestry, etc. predominantly require local labour. In NGO's sponsored development projects this labour component is extensively utilised.

Here one needs to distinguish between paid labour and contributory labour. Paid labour refers to exertion of body and mind primarily for earning wages while contributory labour refers to performing a job, predominantly with a social concern, which may or may not complement the person with due wages.

In some projects rural people extend their labour totally free of wages and in many cases for lesser wages.

Here a question may arise, as to why at all people must toil with less wages for more work. While project budget is designed for lakhs and crores of rupees why NGOs need to emphasize free labour participation. Does it not appear as an injustice to the beneficiaries?

In development sense, it is a motivating goad to make the people believe that they are the owners of the project and hence the job is theirs.

CASE STUDY

LABOUR CONTRIBUTION GIVES MORAL POWER TO EACHANGADU WOMAN

The women of Eachangadu (at Pudukkottai District of Tamil Nadu) approached the NGO (CASA) to support them in constructing a day - care centre. After a series of discussion, the Mahalir Sangam (Women's Association) assured that they would extend their entire labour contribution for no wages. Accordingly, the women of each family participated in the construction on a turn-basis. The centre was completed and the noon-meal scheme was introduced by the Government of Tamil Nadu whereby nearly 40 children are benefited.

An interesting incident that happened in the day-care centre helps one understand the legimate right claimed by a mother.

One day the creche teacher sent out a child in the mid-day before the noon-meal time due to his mischievousness. The mother came to the centre to inquire into the matter. The dialogue went on as follows

Mother	What is wrong with my child?
Creche Teacher	He was doing all sorts of mischieves including beating other children.
Mother	Why did you send him out of the centre? Just for that? You could have taken corrective action.
Teacher	He is a problem for other children. I have the right to send him out.
Mother	Now, will you take back the child or not?
Teacher	He cannot find a place in the centre any more.
Mother	Why like that? I say, you will not find a place in this centre. *(The mother shouted).*
Teacher	What are you talking? This is not nice. Mind your words.
Mother	Then, How can you say that my child does not find a place? You know, I have carried on my head the bricks, sand, and cement, for the construction of this day care centre entirely free of wages. Every brick of this centre would say the pain of my labour, so also that of other women. I have my right to get my child admitted into the day care centre. In fact, I have the privilege to say 'you get out of the centre'. *(The teacher was shocked to hear this).*

In the meantime, other women too gathered there and asked the teacher to apologise. The child rejoined with his peers. The matter was reported to the officer-in-charge of the daycare centre who also felt sorry for that.

This incident makes us realise that while people contribute their labour they develop a sense of attachment, ownership and belongingness. They gain a moral command over the programme or project. They also become unpaid caretakers of such project activity. Contract-based constructions are carried out with the hands of the labourers whereas participatory-labour-based constructions like that of Eachangadu community centres are built more by their hearts. This is the impact of participation.

In countries like India, where the labour force is abundant, this could be exploited in a more productive manner. There are voluntary organisations which successfully accomplish many projects through participatory labour. Examples are - CASA, Catholic Multipurpose Social Service Societies, Sarvodhaya Sangams, etc. In many cases their labour is not paid in terms of money but in terms of rice or wheat along with pulses, oil etc. This is called the food for work programme. The principle behind this is that the local infrastructural needs could be accomplished with the participation of the communities and at the same time they gain an employment opportunity to earn their bread. So also, food becomes the tool of community organisation and instrumental to promote co-operation and joint action to carryout other development programmes.

Such programmes have created solidarity among the different groups of people. The village level organiser of such programmes also develops leadership and gains social recognition and reward. It is not an exaggeration to state that the local rural leaders who organised food for work project sponsored by agencies like CASA, have risen up to the position of the Chief Ministers and Cabinet Ministers in the country.

In those days, say in Tamilnadu, people themselves volunteered to reconstruct their channels and tanks on their own initatives every year or as and when required what is called Kudimaramathu (Kudi means people: Maramathu means repair/reconstruct). But those good elements are getting dwindled among the rural communities. NGOs have to revivify and enliven these potential elements for the cause of reconstruction of rural India and uphold companionship in community action. Of course, programmes like Janmabhoomi in Andra Pradesh are massively involving people in reconstructing their infra structures.

4.2 Contribution in Kind

Apart from labour contribution, giving things in terms of materials is another important component of people's participation. For instance, while constructing a community centre people contribute necessary timber for making doors, windows, etc. For works like deepening of pond etc., people use their tools and implements like spade, crow bar etc. In programmes like Balwadi (creche) there are villagers who contribute rice, wheat, ragi, maize, millet, pulses, etc., to feed the children. Especially women take active part in such programmes. We can cite instances that the women themselves manage the balwadi without any outside teachers or external support. Suppose there are 30 children in a centre the mothers take care of cooking food etc., on rotation basis, either individually or jointly with one or two.

4.3 Contribution in Cash

Villagers collect cash contribution for many public activities. Invariably we find that the people collect contributions from each family for celebrating temple festivals, Manju Virattu (bull-fight) etc. In the projects sponsored by the NGOs, a small portion is being mobilised from the people as cash contribution. People voluntarily contribute their cash component in projects like community well, horticulture, social forestry etc. They may procure sand for construction, purchase seedlings etc., at their own cost while other support could be made available from the NGOs. Tools and implements like pick-axe, crow bar, spade, pulley etc. that are required for projects are also purchased by the people with the assistance of the NGOs and the same are converted as assets of the local Sangams which can be let out on hire after the proposed project is completed.

More particularly during the asset creation like purchase of milche animals under Government schemes the beneficiaries additionally have to bear upto 20% of its cost to select a better hybrid animal.

It is also widely seen that DWCRA groups and SHGs save their money, lend the same to their members and carryout many women development programmes of their own.

Thus in villages one can observe labour, kind and cash as participatory components to a great deal in NGO's sponsored programmes.

CASE STUDY

NO WOMEN - NO PONGAL

People in villages generally extend more participation towards festivals, merrymaking and jubiliant occasions than for a development cause. A peculiar case study is given here for reference.

In a village at Sivaganga District in Tamil Nadu an initiative was taken by the women to construct a creche with the help of a Voluntary Organisation. The Agency convened a village meeting, and worked out a building plan. The design constituted two portions — one for the creche and the other for common purposes like training, employment programmes etc. The total cost was estimated at Rs. 1 lakh. To ensure people's participation the Agency called for 10% contribution (Rs. 5000 as cash contribution and the remaining Rs. 5000 as labour from the village). On hearing this in the meeting, the men folk grumbled and asked why the people should contribute while the Agency was getting foreign money. The women remained silent which expressed their concern and consent. In a male dominated village like that women could not resist men's view openly. However some of the women tried to assure that they could contribute something on their part. But the men interrupted, and acridly abused them that they were not competent to decide such things and asked them to keep quiet.

Meanwhile, some men appeared very smart and advised the development worker to modify the plan. They suggested that instead of constructing a building worth of Rs. 1 lakh they could reduce the size and complete the centre within Rs. 90,000 so that the question of people's contribution would not arise.

The development worker smiled at them and tried to convince that it was not the question of money but the question of people's involvement (which is a must and also the first and foremost requirement in any development process). In turn, the men jeered at the C.D. worker. The seriousness of the meeting was diluted and the men slowly dispersed. However the women group remained there and discussed about the construction of the creche which would take care of their children when they went out for farming and other activities.

The development worker re-assured them that the organisation could support them in constructing the creche only if the people extended their contribution. The women group then worked out their action plan. Few days passed.

The village people were getting ready to celebrate the Pongal festival. Pongal is a popular festival in Tamil Nadu and Southern states which is celebrated immediately after harvest. Pongal is cooked in the newly bought mud pots with the rice harvested afresh and people offer prayers to Sun God for prosperity.

Accordingly the Pongal day was dawn. Children put on their new clothes. The mike set was switched on. The cattles were decorated. All the men and children thronged into the temple premises. But surprisingly no women reached there to cook/prepare the Pongal. The men announced in the mike and called on all the women to come to the temple to cook Pongal rice. But the women turned deaf ears and remained at home. The men who were overwhelming with joy in carnival moods and tumultuous joy were perplexed as to why no women came there. The men felt that something had gone wrong. Some of them told, "We, men, ourselves can cook Pongal". Many of them told, that if there be **No Women's participation, No Pongal festival at all.** They sent their children to call their mothers. It was learnt through them that the women were worried over the fact that the men, who were collecting so much of money for Pongal and Bull-fight, were not interested in the construction of a creche which was most essential to care the infants in the village.

They sent words that they would not turn up to cook Pongal unless the villager's contribution of 10% for the creche was finalised. The men were upset upon the action on the Pongal eve. They were amazed how these women had privily planned this. The elders of the village advised the men that the women's stand was genuine and hence their request might be considered.

Accordingly, men agreed to the women's proposal. Followed by that, the Pongal pot overflew.

(Few more case studies highlighting People's participation in community health, lift irrigation etc., are incorporated in the Chapter entitled "Specialities of NGOs' interventions in rural development").

5. RESULTS OF PARTICIPATION

Effective people's participation may sometimes become a challenge for governments and vested interests who may feel that their traditional power base can be undermined by the promotion of popular people's participation. Some people also voice the concern that participation may sometimes give rise to expectations that cannot be fulfilled. However, there are several convincing arguments in favour of peoples participation in development.

5.1 Efficiency

Participation allows for more efficient use of resources available for a project or programme. For example, participation helps minimize misunderstanding or disagreements and thus the time and energy often spent by professional staff in explaining or convincing people may be reduced. Participation also proves cost effective when people take responsibility.

5.2 Effectiveness

Participation allows people to have a voice in various stages of project formulation and management. Their local knowledge, resources and skills are used which results in more effective projects.

5.3 Self Reliance

Participation helps to break the mentality of dependence and helps to promote self awareness and confidence, which allows people to analyse their problems and think of positive solutions.

Participation is concerned with human development. It increases people's sense of control over aspects which affect their lives and helps them learn how to plan and implement and on a broader front prepare them for participation at regional and even at national level.

5.4 Coverage

Most of the government directed projects reach only a small and generally privileged number of people. Participation helps to bring more people within the direct influence of the development activity. It increases the number of people who potentially can benefit from development and also helps to draw the voluntary services of the beneficieries in specific and the masses in general. That is why NGOs are by and large involved in Government sponsored projects to take care of social components and community organisations. This is because the NGOs are experienced and competent to elucidate participation.

5.5 Sustainability

It has been seen that externally motivated development projects generally tend to fail once the initial level of support is reduced or withdrawn. Participation ensures that the local people maintain and sustain the project even after withdrawal of the external agency. Professional NGOs consult and involve people right from the planning process applying PRA techniques.

A more detailed study of fifty-two USAID projects found a strong correlation between participation and project success, especially when participation took place through organization created and managed by the beneficiaries themselves (World Bank, 1992).

6. A CRITIQUE

People's participation is a 'fashionable term' that is being used from the gross root workers upto the development magnates sitting in the internationally reputed organisations like the U.N.

In the NGO's context, no project proposal is designed without the catching phrase "People's Participation".

Once approval is accorded some of the executives in NGOs *forget the very "strategy and concept of participation" and adopt "convenient strategy of participation" conducive to their existence and growth.*

In case of non-professional NGOs it is observed that only a conditional participation is invited. More the people participate less would be the say on the part of the NGOs. They are internally happy to keep the people as participatory dependents of the NGOs rather than voluntary or motivated participators of development.

Between people and NGOs, the local leaders sometimes become an intermediary and they want to claim that they are the key stake holders in development of the people: but for them, development would not occur.

In some cases the people become the passive recipient actors. They are content as they get something atleast.

In the context of projects, it is worth analysing critically certain styles of 'so called participation' in the development process. This may help NGOs to facilitate genuine participation.

6.1 Non - participatory participation

This would refer to programmes in which people are not mentally and socially involved but for mere wages or tiny tips. "Taking part" has already been mentioned as participation. Bullocks too are engaged for example, in pulling the cart, and for transportation of the produce from the field to the nearby market. But the bullocks do not know why they are pulling the cart, what are loaded in the cart, to what destination they are engaged, at what time they reach the market and when they will return to the pinfold. Yet for all, the bullocks are used in all the processes of the work.

Similarly in a development programme in certain cases, people are left unaware of the objectives of a particular project, the contents, schemes, and the anticipated impact. This is more true in the top-down approaches adhered to by some NGOs.

The focal point here is that without an inner urge or drive or motivation or enthusiasm or interest or initiative the real participation cannot happen though people are used or engaged in a given project.

People's participation can neither be plucked off nor pressurised to gratify the needs of the implementing agencies. The truth is that people's participation must evolve from the planning process. Participatory development is more a psycho social exercise of the people themselves.

6.2 Hypocritic Participation

In Indian culture, people usually offer some food to crows before they take any special meal. Keeping the food visible, they may call crows with a sound (like Ka Ka). Crows, on seeing the food gather together to have their share. After that, they flock away in scattered directions. Similarly it is observed that people are/get organised for a particular project activity quickly and suddenly. For any material benefit people may come together unmindful of their time and energy. One cannot blame people because they are deprived of many basic things. But this helplessness of the poor and the downtrodden should not be misutilised by the Government or NGOs to justify their claim that they ensure people's participation. Gathering around charity can not be deemed as participation. It is observed that some raw - NGOs depict video shows and film shows to entice people and to show the same crowd to the funding representatives who come to plan, observe or evaluate the development process.

So also we find more active participation while availing a bank loan or other material assistance than on other occasions. There are instances that people's organisations promoted by NGOs got disorganised, dissolved or liquidated for want of sustainable participation since participation is not deep rooted in the minds of the people right from the initial stage. This is owing to unsystematic intervention on the part of the implementing agencies and personnel.

Hence the development personnel must be very much aware that a process oriented participation needs to be promoted and not a product oriented. Nowadays it is unpleasant to note that in some cases, the Government and some NGOs join hands but ultimately forget the people. Any secret agreement or unwritten treaty between the funding representatives and NGOs will only jeopardise the voluntary sector.

6.3 Participatory Rural Appraisal (PRA)

The practice of the PRA method has been so much popularised and glorified that it is even seen as the ultimate alternative to 'participation from below'. At the practice level, some are not clear about what, in the long run, it is supposed to contribute other than the fanfare this exotic method makes. But, it certainly and increasingly is becoming an acceptable and popular method to the 'external designer' groups - everybody wants PRA to be done in their projects - perhaps because they see it either as a quick or "rapid" way of getting the local communities' acceptance to their (external planners') designs or as a way of "localising, internalising" their externally designed projects. Looking at this way, this method would perhaps seem manipulative.

Hence PRA requires careful and unbiassed facilitation.

It may not be absolutely convincing that participation has clear practical advantages for development projects. Participation may have adverse effect as well. As Oakley *et al.* (1991) points out participation may cause delay, increase cost and gives an opportunity to the people to oppose the project. The World Development Report 1992 also mentions that participation tends to be expensive and can cause or enhance local conflicts by reinforcing the power of local elite by way of decentralizing decision-making (World Bank. 1992).

7. PRINCIPLES OF PARTICIPATION

The major principles pointed out are centrality of people, people's knowledge and resources and involvement of women and other disadvantaged categories of people.

7.1 The Centrality of people

People are central to participatory development. Participatory development intervention must be based on the needs of the people as identified by them, their analysis of issues and their decisions. It also implies an implicit faith that people, irrespective of their condition of poverty and oppression, can progressively transform their environment with the help of, but not dominated by, external agents. In essence, participatory development demands that common and subaltern populace should move from being objects to becoming subjects of development projects and programmes. Any effort to promote popular participation should strengthen local capacity and mobilize local resources.

7.2 Local Knowledge and resources

A major corollary to the people - oriented, people centred and participatory development is the principle that people's knowledge or local knowledge should be given primacy in development action. Attempt to undermine people's knowledge will never create a condition in which the target people can associate themselves with the project.

People have many alternative solutions for their problems. In fact, NGOs must unlearn what they have learnt but learn things from the people to sort out participatory strategies.

7.3 Involvement of women and other marginalised categories

A third fundamental principle of participatory development emphasises the marginalised categories including women as equal partners in the process of development. This principle is, to a large extent, a reaction to a dominant feature of other development strategies. In other words the poor, impoverished, Dalits and women folk should be offered just and due opportunities in decision making, community action, community leadership, community management etc.

Besides these three broad principles, there are other principles which are related to specifiic projects and programmes directed at specific social groups, communities and categories. As far as the project is concerned, it should have clear objective ensuring distributive justice and continuing benefits to the people.

8. CORE ELEMENTS OF PARTICIPATION

Participation is people's business since people are/should be the primary actors in development. Peopleparticipate more in the relevant programmes that concern them.

People's participation cannot be plucked off or pressurised but it must evolve.

Participation should not be conditioned. The same must be allowed to emerge and develop. Participation cannot be a sudden intervention at the convenience of the external forces like NGOs or the Government. It must originate from and within the people and the implementing agencies can facilitate to arouse the same systematically and strategically.

If development work initiates people's participation the same will ensure a successful development.

Participation cannot be a favour to the people from the side of the NGO or the Government but it is people's legitimate right. Participation must promote people's empowerment.

The arguments on participation seem to converge on the relationship between two key concepts viz. 'taking part' and 'influence'. Moreover, any participation process seems to have two components irrespective of the context, situation or objective: (a) a decision-making process to realise the objective decided upon; (b) an action process to realise the objective decided upon. Participation may be partial when one of them is absent. In the former, participation may mean 'taking part to decide' and in the latter 'taking part in the carrying out'. This meaning holds good for the situation in which all the participants are socio-economically equal and, consequently, equal in the ability to influence decision making. But when the participants are unequal in thier endowments, participation means 'taking part by the less-endowed to influence the decision-making process in their favour and in the carrying out of the outcome'. Taking part essentially then means the collective actions of the less endowed. Stiefel's (1981:1-2) view of participation as an "organised struggle of the poor for more favourable terms of incorporation and for improved prospects" seems very relevant here. Participation of the poorest in this sense will entail a socio-political process.

Concluding Remarks

Hence Development sans people's participation means Development Sans Development.

8

Advocacy

ADVOCACY MEANS INFLUENCING POLICY
IN FAVOUR OF THE POOR AND POWERLESS
THIS OTHERWISE, MEANS
A MISFAVOUR TO THE POWER HOLDERS

The emerging role of NGOs is nothing other than advocacy. The advocacy role by NGOs has become a crying need in the current context of market economy. However much NGOs carry out service delivery and socio-economic development programmes with commitment, development of the poor and the powerless becomes partial, incomplete transitory and fleeting unless policies are made in favour of them. This could be achieved through advocacy.

Traditionally non-government organisations (NGOs) have mostly focussed their attention on grass-root action, ignoring the larger environment in which they operate. But more recently due to fundamental changes in the country's economic and political environment, NGOs have been forced to realize seriously the role of macro level forces shaping the micro level realities. Although advocacy is new, the practice has been there much longer. Advocacy in India has its roots in the work of Raja Ram Mohan Roy, Mahatma Gandhi etc. Several government policies including the abolition of Bonded Labour Act (1976) and the primary health care policy were influenced by the work of NGOs.

Nevertheless, much needs to be done on the emerging advocacy role by NGOs as a systematic endeavour, an organised activity, a strategic attempt and collective action to influence policies. The concepts and strategies of advocacy substantiated by case studies and NGO's experiences, are dealt with in this chapter to facilitate NGO persons to internalise and perform the same.

In fact, NGOs by and large need to learn a lot about advocacy and the art of exercising advocacy role. Hence this chapter is designed to equip the readers with the concept of advocacy, tactics for successfully carrying out advocacy, understanding policy and strategies of performing advocacy roles in influencing policy, dos and don'ts in advocacy etc.

1. DEFINITION

(i) Advocacy can be understood as a delibrate, organised and systematic effort to influence policy affecting the poor, marginalised, unprivileged and the disadvantaged.

(ii) A series of actions designed to persuade and influence those who hold governmental, political and economic power so that they will formulate, adopt and implement public policy in ways that benefit, strengthen and improve the lives of those with less conventional political power, and fewer economic resources. Advocacy should change societies, institutions and power relationships. (ADVOCACY INSTITUTE).

(iii) Influencing decision makers to design, adopt, and change policies and practices in furtherance of our mandate (OXFAM).

Organizing informations into arguments to be communicated through various inter-personal and media channels with a view of getting political and social leaders' acceptance, and preparing a society for a particular development programme. (UNICEF)

Advocacy is defined as a deliberate, organised and systematic effort to influence public policy (drawn up at the Advocacy Workshop in December 1992 by Action Aid India). Advocacy is a strategy available for NGOs to add to their usual strategy of operational programmes.

Few notable NGOs in the country have articulated their role on advocacy and released bulletins and publications to offer conceptual clarity for their own staff members and others. Agencies like ACTION AID, India have made a pioneering attempt to popularise the concept of advocacy among partner agencies and other NGOs by organising various workshops apart from releasing series of issues on advocacy.

2. CONCEPT OF ADVOCACY

The term 'advocacy' means different things to different people. Advocacy is used to mean everything from street protests to publication of research reports.

The theatres where advocacy shows are held vary from the Tahsildars' office, to the chambers of the Prime Minister, the corridors of Parliament, the General Assembly of the United Nations and the World Trade Organisation.

Aiming at influencing somebody is advocacy. This 'somebody' is associated in the context of public policy. The public policy emanates from institution of the state and has been defined - somewhat enigmatically - by Thomas Dye, a leading scholar on policy analysis as **"whatever governments choose to do or not to do."**

NGOs have to critically analyse whether the Government policies are pro-poor or not. Many NGOs like DISHA, Ahmedabad read between lines the budgets of the State and the Central Governments since budgets are the manifestations of their policies. Such NGOs facilitate the Opponent Assembly/Parliament members to raise appropriate questions to seek remedial action.

Advocacy can be directed not only towards the Government but also to the implementing institutions that are floating and violating implementational norms laid down by the Government.

"Advocacy is a long distance race. It requires a long-term vision, yet with achievable and measurable goals.

Advocacy is like a war, albeit a bloodless one. Its outcome is rarely decided by the fortunes of one battle. There are a series of battles - from trying to raise awareness about an issue to mounting pressure by getting the media to write about it, getting prominent personalities to talk about it; to lobbying MPs/MLAs to legislate on it, to get the bureaucracy to implement it and then following up to ensure that there is no roll-back. The biggest challenge in all this is endurance. "Successful advocacy requires organisation, tolerance, patience and enthusiasm for the tedious and mundane tasks. It requires building on small victories, sharing credit, learning from defeats and keeping one's eyes focused on the longer-term horizon," argues the Advocacy Institute.

A question that social advocates often encounter is: Isn't advocacy political? Advocacy is no more political than development itself. It is about changing power relationships or as Cochen puts it "enabling those with less conventional political power and fewer economic resources acquire a greater share of both". Advocacy, says Cochen, is committed to using the "instruments of democracy".

The finest example of this, and indeed, the finest advocate this country has produced, is Mahatma Gandhi and his non-violent struggle against colonial rule.

CASE STUDY

GETTING ELECTRIC POWER CONNECTION

In Mithariaya village of Bikaner district in Rajasthan, the folks were denied electric power connection as they had not voted for the local legislator in the election. Several representations made by the villagers to local electricity officials proved futile. Then, according to the story reported in the newsletter of the Consumer Unity & Trust Society (CUTS), one Mahendra Singh Shekawat, a local youth, took the advice of CUTS and rallied the villagers to write five postcards a day to the chairman of the state electricity board at his home address. The transformer which was previously denied to the villagers was soon restored.

A simple story of people's power teaches useful lessons. There are several elements that stand out.

Firstly, the existence of a common problem.

Secondly, the leadership provided by Shekawat.

Thirdly, the people coming together to do something about the problem.

Fourthly, the identification of the target (i.e.) the Chairman of the state electricity board and;

Finally, the choice of the tool/tactic i.e. the simble postcard. It was a deliberate decision to send the postcards to the residential address, rather than to the office, for greater impact.

The above case study demonstrates that advocacy can be effectively practised at the grassroot level by using the simplest of tools. This is not to suggest that a postcard campaign will be effective in solving all rural problems. Also most advocacy issues tend to be more complex than demanding a transformer.

Those relating to matters of influencing government policy require making an indepth analysis of the problem as to its causes and solutions, an understanding of the system and of decision-makers and processes, identifying possible allies and securing their support, engaging a multiplicity of targets at different levels -- village, block, district, state, national and international -- and using a variety of tactics spanning public education, persuasion, litigation and confrontation. Advocacy of this nature and scale demands a systematic and organised approach, particularly as the desired change often comes incrementally and over a long period of time.

3. Elements and Tactics of Successful Advocacy

There are several elements that go to make a successful advocacy strategy.

(i) The First and foremost is the existence of a problem.

No advocacy is possible, or necessary, without there being a problem. The problem in Mithariaya village was straightforward: the denial of electricity because of the grudge of the local legislator. But not all problems may be as simple or as apparent. There is often considerable confusion over "issues" and "problems". Low literacy may be an issue, but the problem could be that of low enrollment, high dropouts, high teacher absenteeism and poor quality of teaching. Of these high teacher absenteeism may be best resolved through advocacy at the local level, while improving the quality of teaching may be more of a teacher training question. Not all problems have their answers in advocacy.

(ii) Leadership is another key element

Several major campaigns such as the Chipko movement and the Narmada Bachao Andolan have been characterised by the leadership, often of the self-sacrificing variety. But where there is no single clear leader, problems do arise in terms of several leaders, particularly in a coalition, competing to don the mantle. One approach that is recommended in such cases is to delay the leadership issue and focus instead on the tasks to be performed. Over time, the leader will emerge naturally from among those who maintains a sustained interest in the issue and perform the tasks assigned to them.

(iii) The next important element is information

Information is required at two levels -- on the problem itself and on the system. NGOs engaged in advocacy typically rely on field information, which is itself largely anecdotal, to frame their arguments. Such information, while useful, is rarely adequate for effecting policy changes at a macro level. Influencing policy makers require a broader information base brought out of research and analysis. Equally important is an understanding of the system. Which is the key decision-making body? What are its powers and functions? What are its rules and procedures? Who is the key decision-maker? Who has the maximum influence on the decision maker? Where/When is the decision-maker most vulnerable? and so on.

(iv) Framing the issue is another important element of an advocacy strategy

Thus an instance of police atrocity against a tribal woman could well be framed as being part of the larger problem of increasing police brutality against poor women. Framing the specific act of brutality in terms of the wider problem is often important to secure lasting solutions. In case of police atrocity case, the demand should perhaps go beyond calling for the suspension of the guilty police official and compensation for the victim and also pressurising the authorities to introduce a course on gender sensitisation in the police training curriculum. The advantage in framing an issue in broad terms is that it then attracts the support of people who may not be positioned to respond to the immediate problem, but have a stake in the wider problem. "Whatever be the campaign or project, that must have a goal big enough to motivate people targeted on the issue".

(v) The setting of objectives is often a logical next step to the framing of the issue

Objectives need to be, as far as possible, SMART -- Specific, Measurable, Achievable, Realistic and Time bound. Thus, to use the above example, suspension of the guilty policeman and compensation for the victim say in three months could be the short-term goal, introduction of the gender sensitisation course in two years the medium term goal and a 50% reduction in police atrocities against women over the next five years, the long-term goal. The importance of short-term objectives is underscored by the Advocacy Institute which says that people will "stay involved if they see that the campaign is producing some worthwhile and visible results in the short-term (six months to a year)".

The launch of a major advocacy effort must almost necessarily be preceded by looking within to see whether the problem falls within the mandate of the organisation. Organisational considerations would involve doing a SWOT analysis including resources available for the effort (money, staff, skills, etc.)

Coalitions are often required, particularly when the issue would require a broad-based and sustained struggle. Coalitions are important as they provide strength of numbers and resources (both financial and human) and also draw public and political support. Confrontation is a tactic that is quite popular with trade unions and other mass organisations which organise public demonstrations, boycotts, etc.

(vi) Another key element in an advocacy strategy is the target

This could be a key decision-maker within the executive, legislature and/ or judiciary in the case of the government, or, in the case of a company, it could be the managing director who is the key decision-maker.

Target is always a person and is never an institution or elected body (Midwest Academy, 1991). This is because the decision makers are individuals and not institutions/organisations. A target could again be classified into primary targets and secondary targets. A primary target is the person(s) who has the power to make the decision while a secondary target is the person(s) who can influence the primary target. A newspaper editorial writer is a secondary target. It is rare in matters relating to framing of public policy that the activist can directly influence the primary target without using secondary targets.

Also in the realm of persuasion is lobbying which requires meeting the target and trying to persuade him/her to a given point of view. Lobbying is not an easy task. It requires a sound understanding of the issue, knowledge of official procedure, background information on the individual being lobbied, finding the right "hook" for each person, etc.

Targets could also be influenced through public education campaigns that seek to bring the weight of public opinion to ear on them. Raising questions in the legislature is another tactic to both raise public awareness on a problem and to pressurise the ruling party.

(vii) Another contributing element is NGO's own strengths/opportunities

Most NGOs have one or more key strengths/opportunities they can capitalise on. In the case of the Narmada Bachao Andolan, for instance, its mass base is perhaps its most important strength; in the case of Adithi, an NGO that works in Bihar, its work being located in an area where the shocking practice of female infanticide is rampant presents a key opportunity; for SEARCH, an NGO working with tribals in Gadchiroli district of Maharashtra and specialising in health issues, its key strength is that the husband and wife team running it are both qualified doctors.

Thus for the Narmada Bachao Andolan, mass rallies, dharnas, etc. that take place from time to time are important to gain/reinforce credibility both among supporters and opponents alike. Similarly in the case of Adithi, the publishing of detailed research with case studies of households practising female infanticide in its area has been important for decision makers to take it seriously. In the case of SEARCH, writing articles on local health problems in leading medical journals such as Lancet, International Journal on Gynaecology and Obstertrics, World Health Forum, WHO Bulletin, etc. appears to have been important in gaining respect.

4. MEDIA ADVOCACY

Use of the mass media is an essential part of any advocacy strategy. The radio, press and television help keep an issue alive and build popular support for it. The creation of media events is often necessary to attract media attention. Mass demonstrations and direct actions make for excellent media coverage and help raise public awareness on an issue. But it is equally important to identify in newspapers and broad-cast through T.V./Radio/e-media because these media opinions are valued by key decision makers.

In India, the press has a natural affinity with the pressure groups due to its long association with the freedom struggle.

News is published free of charge in getting the message across.

Editorials are important as they tend to be read carefully by decision makers. Here again it is essential to establish contact with the editorial writers in newspapers/magazines and keep them informed of the issues.

For instance, as part of an effort to create awareness and generate a debate on the World Food Summit held in Rome 1996, ACTIONAID India got an article published in The Economic Times newspaper. Of course, there were many a writing and editorial in many leading newspapers opposing WTO conference held at Seattle during Dec. 99 for impossing labour and environment standards.

Although India is quite heterogenous, there are some core values that Indians respond to positively. These include family, health, security and freedom. (At the same time there are some negative values such as greed, deceit, corruption, dependency, etc. which evoke a negative response.) A campaign could in its media advocacy try to associate one or more positive values.

Press lines are particularly important for TV and radio news interviews where coverage is likely to be restricted to three or four quotes. This is the age of the "media bite" which is nothing but short and pithy quotes that encapsulate both information and effective symbols for an audience that is increasingly used to getting its information in short bursts.

Preparing a standard press kit containing "evergreen material" such as a brochure on mission, goals and services, relevant statistics relating to the issue, etc. is important for media advocacy. Press release should be developed as needed and sent out with the standard press kit.

Finally, it is important for a compaign or an NGO to have a spokesperson trained to articulate the key messages in the manner in which the campaign is framed.

Working with the media may at times be a difficult job. There is no guarantee of coverage or getting the prominence of coverage one may wish. There is also the problem of distortion of the message. But with adequate planning and a clear media management strategy it is possible to make the media a campaign ally.

Building a popular base to an advocacy effort is central to social advocacy. Sometimes policy change can be effected by personal equations an activist may have with the target.

The role of the citizens is the mighty endeavour in shaping the society. The then Indian President Shanker Dayal Sharma quoted that "Let us appreciate that citizenship itself is an office," He told the nation in his Independence Day (1995) eve address that, the ultimate and the greatest power is with us as citizens. That power has to be exercised.

5. WHAT IS A POLICY?

As discussed earlier, this is something which emanates from institutions of the state and has been defined by Thomas Dye, as "whatever governments choose to do or not to do".

A policy is a plan of action, a statement of ideals and a course of action proposed and adopted by a Government or a politcal party or business or a person.

Usually, policies are made in favour of the policy - makers and not pro-poor. That is why there is a wider scope for NGOs to effect a change in the policy to be benevolent to the impoverished.

6. WAYS TO INFLUENCE POLICY

In a parliamentary democracy like India, there are two dominant routes or ways of influencing the public policy.

The first is the route of influencing **decision makers,** through influencing bureaucrats and officials. In this route, study, documentation, analysis, research, workshops, conferences etc. play a significant role.

The second route is influencing public policy by organized interest groups or pressure groups. This is the ***political route*** *where raising one's voice on certain issues in an organized fashion influences the political aspects of public policy. Influencing Parties, Ministers, Members of Parliament and Legislature, Media, Public opinion, etc., are ways of approaching this route.*

In recent years, several issues of the people have been raised in a manner resembling the second route of influencing public policy. If one examines the way women's groups are organised and lobbied for women's rights, if one looks at the manner in which the issues of the alternative legislation for the rights of construction workers has been handled for the last few years, if we look at the ongoing struggles around the issues of tribes' rights on forest, the issue of dams, then we see that the political route to influencing public policy has been attempted.

7. RECOGNITION OF SHGS

Recognition of self-help groups by NABARD is a classical example of influencing the Government policy. Many NGOs for over a score of years organised thousands of self-help groups in the villages.

Having promoted numerous self-help groups in the country NGOs could influence the government with the result that the unregistered self-help groups are also recognised. *Accordingly NABARD, (the apex body of the Indian Banking for rural development), has instructed all the banks to extend credit two or three times more than that of the savings mobilised by the SHGs. The amount lent by Banks is being refinanced by NABARD.* ***It is a glory to the powerless women groups and victory to NGOs who strive to empower them.***

In this regard MYRADA and many other voluntary organisations deserve a special mention in influencing the Government policy.

8. PUBLIC INTEREST LITIGATION

Public Interest Litigation became a popular supportive intervention to strengthen the work of NGOs in influencing, implementation and development of public policy in the early 80's. The main advantage of

Public Interest Litigation is to create the possibility that NGOs and others could approach the Courts for legal justice to the poor. This was made possible by some path-making judgments by the Supreme Court of India, particularly with respect to the issue of release of bonded labour based on the petition of Bandhua Mukti Morcha. The judgment delivered in 1984 led to a widespread recognition of the possibility of using PIL to support struggles on payment of minimum wages. Effective use of Public Interest Litigation was made to push the government and its various agencies to follow its own legislations. In issues related to land ownership and alienation, minimum wages, bonded labour, rights of construction workers and landless agricultural labourers, atrocities on Scheduled Castes and Scheduled Tribes and women and many other related issues, Public Interest Litigation has been effectively used.

CASE STUDY

DISHA'S EXPERIENCE

DISHA is the acronym for Development Initiatives for Social and Human Action. It is registered under the Bombay Public Trusts Act. It was founded in March 1985 and started its work from 1986 by :

(a) Organising forest-labourers such as daily-wage earners employed by the Forest Department of the Gujarat State, and
(b) Organising tribal women working as tendu-leaf plucker.

Disha was formed with the conviction that unless the poor themselves are organised, it is difficult to influence the policies of the government in favour of the poor. Disha is a public trust formed with the broad objective of helping the poor acquire necessary skills, confidence and capabilities to organise themselves for their own development. The idea was to work as a supportive core group for a network of people's organisations at the village level.

Disha has been instrumental in the formation of about a dozen groups including trade unions of agricultural labourers and forest workers in the predominantly tribals living districts of Sabarkantha, Panchmahals and Banaskantha of North Eastern Gujarat. Over the years, the leaders of these groups and trade unions have grown as community leaders of their respective areas. The network of organisations of the poor has emerged as a pressure group which has been able to influence the state administration.

Disha, through these organisations, could pressurise the state administration to take notice of the various problems confronting the tribals and the poor such as their exploitation by the Forest Department, Revenue Department and police officials, rampant corruption in the implementation of various anti-poverty programmes etc., and force the administration to take remedial measures.

A major achievement of the trade unions formed by Disha has been in securing higher wages for the minor forest produce gatherers like tendu leaf plukers and labourers employed by the Forest Department. The trade unions and Gujarat Forest Produce Gatherers and Forest Workers' Union, documented instances of violation of various labour laws and the Minimum Wages Act by the Forest Department fought and secured the same for the labourers due.

In the process of conducting studies of the impact of forest laws on the life of tribals, Disha documented instances of atrocities on the tribals by the forest and police officials as violation of human rights. A study was also made on the impact of the state's annual budget on tribal development whereby it was noticed that the lion's share of the state's spending was on administrative expenses and only a minuscule fraction reached the poor.

The various village-level groups supported by Disha have emerged as pressure groups on local and state administration. A significant achievement of these groups, particularly those of women, is that they liberated the poor from the clutches of money-lenders and redeemed their lands and ornaments.

Significantly, Disha has emerged as an intervention agency on behalf of the tribals and the downtrodden by taking up cases of injustice, violation of human rights and exploitation. Through documentation, public interest litigations, lobbying through newspapers, organising rallies and demonstrations and even holding discussions with government officials, Disha was able to get justice for the tribals, increased wages and the right to cultivate forest lands.

(i) The Case of Purposeless Land Acquisition

In this case some 29 tribals' land was being acquired by GIDC in Banaskantha district. For these tribals the land was their only means of survival. Disha came to know about this. The NGO approached the concerned authorities and the government and asked them to stop acquiring the tribals' land. For almost a year the matter remained at a stand still. Suddenly the land acquisition officer informed these tribals that they were coming to take possession of the land. The NGO immediately approached the High Court for a stay order since at that time there was a standing crop in the land. During the hearing the Judge asked the GIDC officer to hand over their files in this regard. He found a letter saying that they had dropped the acquisition. On seeing this, the Judge asked GIDC whether they had ever dropped the idea of acquiring this land, to which the concerned officer said 'no'; The Judge straight away issued a stay order and also ordered that until and unless they get permission of the High Court they should not acquire this land in future. Thus the 29 tribals' land has been saved from acquisition by the GIDC.

(ii) Payment of Wages - Without Litigation

Another case is related to a marble (stone) factory which had not paid wages to the labourers. This was brought to the notice of the same NGO. Based on this DISHA communicated to the factory owner that the same labourers under their guidance had moved the court on the issue of pending payment of wages. Immediately an amount of Rs. 62,000 was paid in cash to the labourers and they requested that the complaint be withdrawn.

9. DOS AND DON'Ts OF ADVOCACY FOR NGOs

(i) Choosing Advocacy as your strategy

Do link your advocacy work to the main work of your organisation - i.e. something that you know about.

DON'T do advocacy unless you can see a way that it will reinforce the main work of your organisation.

(ii) Specific Objectives

DO set out specific objectives for your advocacy work which you think you can accomplish.

DON'T think that presenting arguments by itself is advocacy.

(iii) Message

DO simplify your message so that it can be clearly understood.

DON'T have an unclear message which will confuse people.

(iv) Targets

DO research and identify the key people or organisations which can influence the desired change.
DON'T scatter your energies.

10. SKILLS THAT NGOs NEED FOR EFFECTIVE ADVOCACY WORK

(i) Organisational ability to :

— see the implications of grass-roots work for policy issues;
— translate grass roots experience into policy pressures.

(ii) Analytical skills to research the situation of :

— the whole community;
— the whole country;
— government priorities/policies;
— international pressures.

(iii) Communication skills to :

— document information clearly;
— package information for different audiences;
— work with the media.

(iv) Readiness and ability to make contacts :
— with potential allies;
— with potential partners;
— with godfathers/godmothers for protection.

11. STRATEGIES FOR NGOs IN ADVOCACY WORK

(i) Think long-term
"advocacy is a long distance race".

(ii) Think wider

"Whatever campaign or project you begin with must be about a goal big enough to motivate people to make your effort a priority".

(iii) Find new allies

"Make strategic alliances and coalitions for bargaining, negotiation, and compromise".

(iv) Consider a variety of tactics

Public education, persuasion, litigation, confrontation.

(v) Upgrade and update your organisation to be able to take on advocacy work

With different skills, different systems, different organisational set-ups, different resources.

CONCLUDING REMARKS

Thus, advocacy is understood as ranging from protest to filing suit in the court to get the policy transformed in favour of the poor and the marginalised. This is a challenging role for NGOs and it is the need of the hour. Service providing, input distributing, welfare doing, and other traditional roles were deemed to be easier tasks. Advocacy, being a tough exercise requires specialised skill.

Every action has its own reaction. In fact, when NGOs promote their advocacy intervention, the reactions may become manifold. Influencing policy in favour of the poor implies a misfavour to the power-mongers. Hence, NGOs may be entangled into the political mire and bureaucratic whips unless advocacy is carried out professionally and strategically.

There are many a Gordian knot against the disadvantaged. To untie or to cut it across, people need to be organised, people's organisations to be net-worked and strategically allied on one hand and NGOs need to work in coalition with other NGOs and allied supporting forces on the other hand.

Advocacy is an innovative and challenging role for NGOs to enable the poor to alter policies in their favour and access control over their resources.

9

Empowerment

WHILE CHARITY MEANS
GIVING SOMETHING TO PEOPLE
EMPOWERMENT SHALL MEAN
GIVING POWER AND AUTHORITY TO PEOPLE

Many NGOs have started to use the term 'empowerment', but clarity is lacking in the understanding of the concept, meaning and the strategies of empowering the marginalised. This chapter is designed to provide the definition and meaning of empowerment, the process involved in empowering the masses substantiated with a few field references and case studies.

In recent years, NGOs give great emphasis to Empowerment. In some NGO premises and training centres one can come across the phrase "From Development to Empowerment". This symbolically represents that NGOs have begun their initiatives in empowering the people.

Building people's organisations is the major contributions of the NGOs in the country and the process of empowerment is gaining momentum through those organisations. NGOs enable the oppressed to unyoke themselves from the clutches of the oppressing. The women, tribals and Dalits who were caught in the web of exploiting elements are able to get themselves released as a consequence of the strenuous works of NGOs.

1. DEFINITION AND MEANING

The term 'empower' is referred to 'to give power or authority to'. NGOs, in the process of development interventions, enable the impoverished and downtrodden to gain power and authority over their livelihood and this is achieved by organising the unorganised sections of the society.

So obviously, empowerment is about power, and about changing the balance of power. In every society, there are powerful and powerless groups. Power is exercised in social, economic and political relations between individuals and groups.

Power itself can be simply defined as control over resources and control of ideology. The resources over which control can be exercised fall into five broad categories:

(a) physical resources (like land, water, forests);
(b) human resources (people, their bodies, their labour and skills);
(c) intellectual resources (knowledge, information, ideas);
(d) financial resources (money, access to money); and
(e) the self (that unique combination of intelligence, creativity, self-esteem and confidence).

Control of ideology means the ability to determine beliefs, values, attitudes - virtually, control over ways of thinking and perceiving situations.

Those who have power are those who control material and knowledge resources and the ideology which govern both public and private life. Thus they are in a position to make decisions which benefit themselves. The extent of power of an individual or group is, in turn, correlated to how many different kinds of resources they can access and control. This control confers decision-making power, which is used to increase access to and control over resources.

"The term empowerment refers to a range of activities from individual self-assertion to collective resistance, protest and mobilization that challenge basic power relations. For individuals and groups where class, caste, ethnicity and gender determine their access to resources and power, their empowerment begins when they not only recognise the systemic forces that oppress them, but act to change existing power relationships".

Empowerment, therefore, is a process aimed at changing the nature and direction of systemic forces which marginalize Dalits, Tribes, women and other disadvantaged sections in a given context".

Thus Empowerment deals with the traditionally suppressed and oppressed socio-economic-political sections of society as stated above.

Empowerment means altering the decision-making process in their favour and ultimately establishing a climate for the exercise of their right to make their own decision in every sphere.

It replaces leadership with representation. It leads to people becoming demanding.

It is a true sense of participation. It means an actual shift of power from the elite to the labourer and also from NGO to people's organisation.

It is a process of self revelation and individualisation.

It is a political process and it ensures self-reliance. Hence can be summed-up by a slogan.

"One for all, all for one and all for all".

2. NGOS' WORK ON EMPOWERMENT

The following factors furnish an understanding of NGO's work on empowerment.

(i) As a Process

Empowerment is not an end product but a process. NGOs understand the *socio-political structure and the environment wherein the powerless people* strive to live. They facilitate the communities to continue their struggle and bargain their rights.

(ii) With a Holistic approach

NGOs work with the poor Communities to a whole range of economic, social and political activities like agriculture, animal husbandry, skill training, adult and non-formal education etc. But all these activities are converging towards the common aim of empowering the poor.

(iii) Related to the Context

Operationally empowerment is understood as a context - specific activity and the same is related to a given local social, cultural, economic and political context.

For instance, Sunderlal Bahuguna organised the village women of

Uttarkand Hills in Uttar Pradesh to protest against deforestaion by embracing or encircling each endangered tree when the woodcutters arrived. Of course, the word Chipko (to stick to, to hug) has since entered the dictionary of environmentalists around the world.

(iv) Organising Marginalised Groups

Empowerment approach is focused on marginalised groups, particularly, the rural poor, women, the landless, the oppressed Dalits, tribals etc. To cite, Bhoomi Sena in Maharashtra works with marginalised adivasis (tribals). Self-employed Women's Association (SEWA), a leading NGO based at Ahemedabad Gujarat, has selected poor women working in the urban informal sectors as its target group.

(v) Aa a Stategic Endeavour

The empowerment approach is chiefly interested in strategic aspects those which are aimed at attacking the fundamental causes of powerlessness. Empowerment implies redistribution of power (which could develop into a "generative" state) between the poor and rich, men and women, caste Hindus and untouchables, etc. It is, therefore, inherently a political process. NGOs with empowerment objectives, consciously or otherwise, aspire to create conditions for incremental structural change from below. This is evident from the experiences of NGOs like CROSS, with an empowerment approach. "Sangams" (groups) are formed not only to struggle for restructuring the ownership of the basic means of production (land) but also to strengthen the base of parliamentary democracy.

(vi) Democratising

India is known for centralisation of socio - political power under various contexts. But the 73rd Amendment is an unique attempt to ensure people's democracy. NGOs enable the communities to execute democracy at the village level, through orientation trainings and other capacity building programmes as discussed in other chapters in the context of Panchayat Raj.

Also the fullest participation is a sign of empowerment. NGOs promote community based organisations wherein a collective leadership and decision making with the involvement of all the members of the associations are facilitated. In the entire course of development interventions, NGOs thrust democratic ideologies.

(vii) Sustainability

Empowering the people means self - reliance. This is possible only when the sangams are able to sustain as a social unit and their projects manageable by themselves. NGOs are very particular in ensuring the same.

The case of working women's Forum (WWF), a South Indian NGO' confirms that sustainability is highly dependent on the adoption of the empowerment approach. WWF encourages womens' groups to design and manage their own projects and activities. The original fund of the Working Women's Cooperative Society provided by donor agencies trebled in size between 1981 — 85 and financial self-reliance has clearly helped in making the programme more sustainable (Azad, 1986).

CASE STUDY

SEWA'S EXPERIENCE IN EMPOWERING THE MARGINALISED WOMEN

ABOUT SEWA

Ahmadabad, the textile mill city, known as Manchester of India, is the birth place of SEWA. Thousands of women were engaged in and around the textile mills as head loaders, hand cart pullers etc. They were paid very low wages and treated at the whims and fancies of their owners and contractors. They were subject to heavy exploitation as they remained unorganized. These voiceless women were watching the activities of the Textile Labour Union (TLA) India's largest Union of textile workers. There are many advantages for the members of the union since TLA could ensure their rights and privileges. Hence a few women, hand cart pullers and head loaders approached the TLA. They were directed to MS. ELA BHATT, a Lawyer who was then heading TLA's women wing. They asked her whether they could get the benefits of the members of such TLA, if they also got together. Though dealing with organized labour, she was constantly exposed to the realities of the poor working class, and the numerous problems of unorganized women workers in India. She realised the felt need of the women to get organized and understood the implied pressure behind their expressions. She enabled the women to join hands and in fact initially two dozen women came together and pooled few paise and took some decisions to demand that their wages to be regularised and that was the day SEWA was born i.e. on DECEMBER 3rd 1971. Soon, used clothes sellers and vegetable vendors wanted to join with them For protection from police buritality and extortion. Then home bound women of the Muslim community who stitch textile waste clothes into garments and quilt covers requested some support. Agricultural workers came to these meetings to discuss how they could actually get the minimum wages they were due under the law. Carpenters and metal smithing women came seeking access to small loans for working capital. Then the exploited beedi workers and incense stick makers joined the union. Women who had migrated to the city for textile mill jobs but had faced retrechment and were reduced to picking recyclable waste from the city's garbages having several ideas to alter their circumstances came to the union for support and services. Weavers, basket makers, block printers etc. facing displacement of their skills or loss of raw materials or markets came seeking help to hold into the only occupations they knew. Women who had been victimised for asking for legal wages in the tobacco processing plants also came seeking legal assistance.

In this way, SEWA grew organically slowly obsorbing more and more trades rooting itself in the reality of poor women. Surprisingly today, in SEWA (after 28 years of existence), more than 50,000 women have joined together.

Outcome and Impact

The felt needs of more than 40,000 have been fulfilled over 28 years.

A social change has been witnessed on the perception of women's right at the community (micro) level and also at the district and state (macro) i.e. in Gujarath and also in the national level. SEWA has found that the only way to bring "Empowerment" is to "Organize, Organize and Organize more women". "In the increasing numbers they have found voice and strength. When they stand in sufficient numbers their voices do shake the power base and change things in their favour right from exploitation of neighbour tender, or local money lender to national and international policies.

The street vendors who provide important daily services squat in the markets with their baskets selling fresh vegetables, fruits, eggs, fish, cooked snacks etc. They were labelled as "encroachers" and their vending was termed as "illegal". They were harassed and beaten by police, their goods confiscated and bribes extorted from the women to let them unharassed for a day or two.

For years municipal authorities and police were not responsive to the SEWA's requests to allocate space and issue licence to these women vendors. Men vendors' families had been selling in the main market for nearly three generations. The women folk decided to take up the matter legally. They took up this case to the Supreme Court. They were successful in getting a ruling in favour of the women hawkers, who now sit with the security of licences. This ruling has also set the stage for the national policy on hawkers and vendors which SEWA is now lobbying to push through Parliament.

The President of India had nominated Ela Bhatt to head the commission on self employed women to study the problems of such women across the country and the report was submitted to Govt. for policy changes.

The then National Front Government appointed Ela Bhatt for the first time as the women member in the planning commission which drafts the five year plans. The agenda of working women had finally won some of the policy attention out of struggling of about 28 years. A solidarity among women, and a "we feeling" is found emerged among women folk.

Women are able to manage their groups and programmes independantly by themselves not only in the community level but also in the federations. Women run health centres by themselves. In the Dairy Cooperatives, women operate their computers for milk testing and accounting.

Women participate in the entire decision making process. Leadership and collective leadership are promoted.

Skills and capacities of women that were latent and hidden were brought out and put to use (e.g.). A carpenter woman Santokbhan by name is now able to operate video camera and produce the video cassets on SEWA programmes.

Poor and marginalised women have become economically sound and socially recognized. (e.g.) SEWA BANK, the bank promoted by the marginalised for the marginalised and of the marginalised women. What the local women admire as their "Mother's Bank", extends credit support to more than 20,000 women every year.

An agriculture labourer NARUBEN by name came to Ahmadebad with Rs. 7.00 only seeking employment. She joined the SEWA co. op. and learnt the skill of sewing and cloth business. Naruben took Rs. 500 as the first loan from SEWA Bank for her business. Over the years, she improved. By 1994, she got 13th loan of Rs. 25,000.

She has now Rs. 30,000 in her fixed deposit and assets worth of

Rs. 20,000 apart from working capital of Rs. 20,000. As an impact of SEWA Bank, a women world bank has been established at Washington following the principles of the former.

3. POWER SHARING

Empowering the people is a STRENUOUS task because it involves power balancing. Sharing of power is the most painful process on the part of power mongers. Power holders like affluents, elites, authorities, industrialists, business magnates, millionaires, popular leaders, bureaucrats, renouned VIPs etc. may be prepared to share a part of their money, a piece of land or any other materials as donations or charities for helping the poor or for constructing a temple or a school etc. But if some one asks for sharing their powers with others, there trigger out the bullets of their self-esteem from their EGO-power gun towards the so-called power-seekers.

Hence NGOs require to facilitate the people with a great deal of wisdom, enormous steadfastness, sustaining perseverance, profound commitment and preparedness for anticipated reactions so as to encounter the situation and to arrive at a more pro-marginalised decision.

Concluding Remarks

If voluntary organisations do not volunteer to empower the poor who else is there to bell the cat?

10

Observation on NGOs — A Swot Analysis

People Predominantly Require

1. Motivation than Money.
2. Awareness than Materials.
3. Information than Inputs Supply.
4. Education than Doles.
5. Empathy than Sympathy
6. Guidance than Gifts.
7. Facilitation than Contribution.
8. Opportunities than Charities.

In this concluding chapter a critical SWOT analysis (Strengths, Weaknesses, Opportunities and Threats) of NGOs in rural development has been made followed by suggestions.

Every NGO is unique in its nature having certain specialities and also with limitations. But there are some commonalities in the strength and weakness among NGOs which are listed out here. Research studies conducted by some reputed Institutions and different individual experts (including the author himself) were drawn as references to make the SWOT analysis.

Strengths

As discussed in Chapter - 4, there are different types of NGOs. Some play mono role and some multiple roles. In general most of the good NGOs have the following strengths:

- NGOs are known for their commitment to serve the poor voluntarily.
- NGO workers are endowed with missionary zeal and commitment. They reach the unreached.
- They are pro-poor and marginalised.
- They live with the people.
- They work for and with the people.
- They work for people's cause altruistically and untiringly. Their work is not clock-bound.
- They are the spokesmen of the marginalised, oppressed, Dalits and women.
  They are the social psychologists to look into the pains and sufferings of the disadvantaged.
- NGO leaders are visionaries of social change.
- They serve the downtrodden unmindful of their pains and inconveniences.
- Upliftment of the poor is their prime motto.
- People are their prime subject matter.
  People's development is their prime objective.
  People's involvement is their paramount concern and
  People's management is their ultimate destination.
- Their plans and programmes are people - centred.
- Their interventions are based on "Caste, Class and Gender - perspectives".
- NGOs are specialists in community organisation.
- They effectively motivate the people to take up their community roles.
- People's participation is the quintessence of NGOs' work.
  Process - orientation is the sine-qua-non of professional NGOs. Target is not their target but the process involved in any programme does matter to them.
- NGOs are well-versed in conducting exercises like PRA (Participatory Rural Appraisal) etc. to draw up information and data from the people and transmit them to the appropriate authorities.
- NGO persons are highly motivated to motivate the unprivileged and

down - trodden.

- They are quicker in decision making.
- They are timely in action.
- NGOs encourage the people that People's development is people's business and facilitate them to do things by themselves.
- NGOs spend a good deal of their time and energy in people's preparedness to ensure that they are psycho - socially equipped to carryout their programmes.
- Good NGOs are governed by high ideals and principles.
- Good NGOs would not compromise to any unethical things. It is a pride for the voluntary sector that certain NGOs do flatly say 'No' to funding agencies if undesirable ideologies are imposed.
- NGOs are strong in their principles. They do not yield to inferior practices.

  For example, a popular NGO in Tamil Nadu has a cattle-feed mixing unit. The feed was sold to farmers at a reasonable price. As per the government's law, sales tax at the rate of 4% was collected from the farmers. The government reduced the rate of sales tax to 3% on a particular month. Unaware of this reduction in sales tax, the unit staff continued to sell, collecting 4% tax and remitted the same amount to the government. This was noticed during checking. The government officials levied a fine of Rs. 15,000 upon the feed mixing unit for the act of collecting excess tax. While the statutory action was on its process on one hand, some elements approached the chief functionary of the NGO to grease their palms with Rs.1,000 i.e. 1/15th of the actual fine so that they could evade the fine. Great thanks and regard to the functionary that he asserted that the organisation would rather be happy to pay Rs.15,000 as fine than a single rupee as a misfavour. The cold elements could not pocket the insult and left the place. The NGO paid the fine as per government's instruction and the feed mixing was set running. This is a good lesson for the other NGOs that whether big or small in size, sound or feeble in funds, long or short in experience, they must stand for the right ends without getting yielded to wrong means.
- Capacity - building is the priority of many NGOs.
- They build people on 'what they know', 'what they have', 'what they are capable of' and 'what they can do' and they do not thrust upon the people which are deemed undesirable.
- They build up leadership qualities even among the nullified sections of the society including women.

- They can enable ordinary people to do extra - ordinary things.
- They have strong will to encounter vested interests.
- They adopt 'bottom-up approach' in their intervention.
- NGOs are competent to sensitise people and create awareness about the root cause of the social inequities.
- Justice to the poor and the oppressed is the linch - pin of issue oriented NGOs.
- NGOs have recently taken up "Gender equality" as one of their main agenda.

  They courageously take-up hard tasks like tackling poverty and injustice.
- NGOs can prevent mighty macro forces from doing injustice to the impoverished in the name of Globalisation, Modernisation, Standardisation etc. by addressing issues and their consequences through lobbying and advocacying.
- They are the ones who build up hopes among the hope-lost poor.
- They organise the unorganised communities and reorganise the disorganised communities.

  NGOs with their committed work prepone development much ahead of its own occurrence.
- They are easily accessible.
- They are the agents of social change. They work for social transformation.

  They identify People's wisdom and incorporate the same for their betterment.
- They believe in people that they can bring about a social change.
- NGOs are the ones who truly empower the people and enable the disadvantaged to access and control over the resources.

  NGOs are the care - takers of the Grass root strata of the society.

  NGOs work to change the policies in favour of the poor.
- NGOs are specialised in social mobilisation. NGOs are with the people. People are with the NGOs. In fact they are both with one another. That is why NGOs have a solemn command over the people and they occupy special room in the hearts of the people. The truth of the fact is that people believe NGOs as the former is the latter's priority.
- However nearer to the people physically, closer to the people mentally, and accessible to the people socially, good NGOs never get diluted and lost themselves. They facilitate the community as a catalyst to accomplish the people's goals.

- NGOs are value centred. They work for constructing a value based society.

Weaknesses

- Although NGOs are committed to their work, they are by and large ill-professional.
- Many NGOs lack clear Vision, Mission and Strategies and hence their interventions become a journey without a destination.
- Benefit supply and Input distribution are still widely prevalent while there is a need for empowering the people.
- NGO means a ONE MAN's SHOW (in many cases).
- It is unfortunate to state that for many NGOs, Money is the prime mover for their interventions. NGOs are in certain cases used as money making platforms. There are few intermediaries and brokers who get project proposals approved on commission basis. How will the commission based projects of NGOs bring about community based development?
- NGOs may work for social justice and equality to the poor. But within the organisations, such things are missing. NGOs tend to take much advantage of its autonomous system.
- Any producer depends upon the customers from whom he has to collect back his investments. The products are checked and tested by him. So he carefully produces, and promptly supplies. But that is not the case with the NGOs. They are not directly answerable to the beneficiaries (to whom they ought to be) because money comes from the other end i.e. donors. Hence in the context of charity, welfare, relief or development or empowerment there is every possibility to take advantage of financial and other resources.
- Accountability and Transparency are found very less among NGOs.
- Management is poor. Many NGOs do not have service rules and regulations. Flexibility is the advantage for NGOs. But too much of flexibility results in too loose administration. NGOs seem to give less importance to personnel management, Human resource development and also in financial management though they are better in project implementation.
- Some NGOs' financial management is like that of **'Penny wise and Pound foolish'**.
- Voluntarism in some cases is found revolving around casteism and nepotism and in certain cases slips into romanticism succumbing to

the collopse of the organisations.

- It is sad to understand that those who fail in every field including politics ultimately reach voluntary sector and pollute the standards of the system.

Tughlak style of administration is not exempted to voluntary organisations too.

- Due to poor monitoring and supervision sometimes staff at the field level are found missing from their field head quarters. Some of them may visit the villages staying in towns far away from the service area.
- Some organisations lack co-ordination between the field workers and the office staff. The workers in the office may feel superior as they are nearer to the resource/power base and can influence the executives easily. So also the field workers feel themselves great because such an office itself exists only due to their work performances. In certain NGOs, it is also observed that nobody is under any body's control. Such things are quite common where PM & E unit or system is absent or weak.

Many NGOs lack internal checks and control in the management of Men, Material, Money and Programme.

In some cases, NGOs are badly affected by political and religious leaders and in few cases by certain extremists.

NGOs sprout and grow within a family, caste groups and religious mates on account of accessibility to resource agencies rather than inspired by any vision.

It is unfortunate to state that the Chief functionary himself/herself happens to become, in some cases, the major beneficiary of the NGOs, as he/she happens to take advantage of all the available materials, infra structural and professional services that are meant to benefit the poor as a consequence of which voluntary sector is looked down upon by the public.

NGOs workers lack a shared Vision and Mission. In certain large organisations when the last person understands clearly the mission, the first person happens to shift and change/modify his mission. Percolation of mission to the down end and internalisation of the same at the lower level do not take place uniformly as a result of which contradictions and confusions are bound to occur among NGO workers.

NGOs may do good field work. But reporting and documentation is summarily poor and in certain cases nil.

Internal and external evaluations are not conducted on a regular basis.

Self-assessment mechanisms are not found in NGOs.

While written bylaws are held in safety lockers, unwritten bylaws, i.e. whims and fancies of the chief executives govern the so called organisations.

In some cases NGOs and Funding partners (local) join together and forget the people for whose cause they have to meet one another.

To get the work done in time, NGOs also grease the palms of the Government regulating authorities like Registrar Office, Income Tax Office, Transport Office etc., who are supposed to fight against corruption pratices.

It is not uncommon that even in certain reputed NGOs 'petty-coat administration' is found to be prevalent which causes blemish to the voluntary sector.

In certain NGOs' intervention the ends appear to be good but not the means.

In some cases NGOs work for more than a score of years creating dependency among the people.

NGOs substitute people's roles which blocks people's action.

In some villages duplication of work is done by different NGOs causing damage to community organisation.

Small NGOs are looked down upon by grown up NGOs. Mutual trust and help are unseen.

NGOs are found to be outmoded in their approach. They do not have the curiosity to look for the current technical and professional advancements which are beneficial to rural development.

Relief and rehabilitation - oriented work and service delivery are still in vogue among the NGOs while there is a crying need for sensitizing the people and empowering the masses.

To a few, NGO means sending proposals. Proposal means funding agencies. Funding agency means project approval, project means gift money and gift money means happy and pompous life. Because of such attitudes of some inferior NGOs, good NGOs are also subject to bad indictment.

Threats

- Every action has its own reaction. For NGOs' work, reactions and THREATS are manifold because of vested interests whose power and authorities are questioned by NGOs' facilitation.

  Some political parties are highly antagonistic towards NGOs. If such parties come to power, there will be a an eclipse upon NGOs. Mushrooming of NGOs results in heavy competition among them which breeds hostile and unhealthy relationships. There exists a kind of virus among them that they undermine and unduly criticize one another. In this way NGOs themselves remain a threat for NGOs. Why do they fail to understand that the rivals' roses will also look pretty with fragrance?

- In the NGO sector, we find two kinds of personalities 1. Bureaucratic, the power mongers and 2. Charismatic developmentalists. The latter, if chronically get frustrated, leave their organisation leaving a vacuum there on the one hand and adding additional competitions and rivalries on the otherhand. This creates rivalry among NGOs and also adds to the proliferation of NGOs.
- Some NGOs carryout activities privily and in isolation. While there is no field base they go on buying vehicles and constructing buildings for their own utility. One day or other these assets will be seized by the authorities or captured by the people.
- In some NGOs formation of union is cropping up, thwarting the functions of voluntarism.
- Fund - raising has become a painful exercise to many NGOs. The trend of foreign funds is slowly dwindling. Of course local funding is upwarding. While certain pseudo NGOs through unethical means raise funds, good NGOs suffer more as they are not prepared to compromise/sacrifice values. Funding to wrong NGOs breeds corruptive practices and commercialisation of voluntary sector. Hence for a few, NGOs means 'Investmentless Business'.
- NGOs have to raise funds from the Government or other sources which are themselves inherently corruptive. If money comes to NGOs from corruptive systems how can they provide clean administration? This is the real problem of many small NGOs who could neither compromise their values nor are they in a position to say 'No' to unclean funding on account of their need for survival and existence.
- As flow of foreign funds is considerably getting lesser and lesser organisations particularly the ones which maintain huge staff structure are already facing enormous financial constraints in sustaining themselves.
- The FCRA for some agencies are even cancelled on account of some vested interests. As NGOs facilitate conscientisation, campaign approach and movement strategy among the masses, the same becomes a threat to the anti-social elements, who, inturn, try to eliminate NGOs

from the scene.

- NGOs work for sustainability of the people's organisation but hardly for themselves. As long as funds flow NGOs go ahead. If money stops, ...??

Opportunities

- NGOs have emerged as a third sector today, next to Govt. and corporate sector. NGOs occupy prominence in every walk of social life particularly in rural development.
- Global forces and market economy pose threats to the poor and marginalized rural masses. These threats and challenges are otherwise opportunities for NGOs to address the issues, awake the people and empower them to protect their interests.
- NGOs have a wider scope to promote Self Help Groups and Micro financing. Both the Central and State Governments encourage NGOs to replicate good models of SHGS, Mahila Banks or federation of SHGS.
- NGOs have much to do in translating SGSY to rural people and enable them to avail the best out of the same.
- International organisations like the U.N. World Bank, and donar countries etc. emphasize, as mandate, to involve NGOs in projects sponsored by them.
- Though Foreign funding directly to NGOs is on a downward trend, specialised Local agencies like CAPART, RMK, SIDBI, Ministry of HRD, Social Welfare, Health, Environment, Forestry and Various other foundations provide a fillip to NGOs' innovative initiatives.
- Disaster preparedness in the coastal villages is yet another area for NGOs to perform their challenging roles.
- Environment is everybody's concern. NGOs have enough opportunities to undertake programmes on environment promotion through innovative projects.
- The rural India as a whole has been classified into Macro and Micro water shed regions and specific plans and budgets have been ear marked under DPAP for Water-Shed-Developments. NGOs are invited to work as Project Implementing Agencies (PIA) which is a wonderful opportunity to make use of the Social mobilisation skill and other competence for the cause of Rural Development.
- 73rd amendment is a wonderful opportunity for NGOs to guide PRIs to ensure grass-root democracy.

- Women development and Gender equality is yet another challenging task before NGOs. For the next twenty years a major thrust would be given on women's development and empowerment. Much and more needs to be done on Gender - sensitisation. NGOs can take up this single entity as their primary task.
- 'Micro finance to the rural poor' by the funding agencies abroad, NABARD, Nationalised Banks, RMK etc., provide greater opportunities for NGOs to experiment and promote sustainable models.
- There is a wider scope for NGOs to carry out community health progrmmes. HIV/AIDS has become an alarming problem in the country. Correct and right kind of messages have not reached the rural men and women. People are frightened than educated. Hence, NGOs can do much in Aids prevention through awareness creation.
- Capacity Building still remains a vacuum among the rural masses. Hence there is a greater need to impart capacities to rurual communities on economic development, community leadership, management of resources, sustaining peoples organisations and their programmes.
- In countries like India, there are numerous Government schemes, like SGSY, DPAP, Community Health, Agriculture Development, Animal Husbandry and so on. But these schemes do not reach the people, timely, justly and fully due to inherent weaknesses in the Government system. Such schemes are like that of an "Operation success but patient died". NGOs can educate and empower Community Based organisations who can best avail the schemes.

Suggestions

- NGOs must first become **THINKING ORGANISATIONS**. Doing things without thinking and critically analysing will bear no sustainable fruits. NGOs must learn to think beyond money, beyond their project, and beyond their own organisations. Being broader and critical in thinking will result in wider and greater impact. Creative thinking, dynamic thinking, critical thinking, fore-sighted thinking, macro level thinking, contemporary thinking/current scenario thinking and eventually people centered thinking are the basic indicators of a good NGO. Their fitness and rightness need to be updated with every day's thinking.
- NGOs' thrust must be on **BUILDING PEOPLE** individually and collectively. The different facets of building people are hope building

among the people, awareness building, knowledge building, skill building, capacity building, confidence building, health building, perspective building, morale building, character building, leadership and collective leadership building, group building, inter and intragroup relationship building, mutual trust building, gender-friendly attitude building, eco-friendly psyche building, unity building, value building etc. Human elements are the pivot around which the entire development interventions should revolve. Any extent of benefit distribution, or input supply or monetary intervention without human building will be a shelter without foundation.

- NGOs have to clearly articulate their Vision and Mission. Orientation must be given to every one of the Board members/staff irrespective of their ranks and position so as to enable them to internalise the organisations' Vision and Mission. Also every one's duties and responsibilities, individually and collectively need to be clearly spelt out to fulfil the purpose of the organisation.
- NGOs by and large, must improve their professional knowledge, skill and competence to meet the needs of the day.
- However genuine or good in work the NGOs may be, they need not function in isolation. They must interact with other related organisations be it NGOs, Govt., Corporate sector, legal bodies, etc.
- There is a crying need for NGOs to seriously look into the impact of "**zations**" (ie) globalization, modernizations, standardization, literalization, industrialization, commercialization, etc., (refer Chapter-1) These modernizations are the threats for poor rural communities who are of their own and who satisfy their needs locally within the available resources. Hence the NGOs have to lay their heads together and think and plan together so that the macro forces do not nullify the vulnerable rural communities. NGOs who are supposed to be pro-poor and people centred must shoulder greater responsibilities firmly, constantly and diligently to work out plans to protect the interest of the poor by lobbying, advocacying or by any other means of empowering the poor masses.
- NGOs need to think globally and act locally.
- 73rd Amendment is a great boon for the Indian rural society particularly for the women folk. But in practice, Panchayats are being governed by benamies. Panchayat representatives do not have competence to plan proposals for the uplift of the village. Hence NGOs can impart training to the Panchayat representatives, particularly women to work out Panchayat development plans, financial

management and other administrations.

- The term 'facilitation' occupies a prominent place in the dictionary of NGOs. But in some NGOs, workers take advantage of the jargon 'facilitation' without understanding the true meaning of it. It is widely spoken that a shift has taken place among the NGOs from doer's role to facilitating role. Facilitation is not doing. But it does not mean escaping from one's own responsibility or skipping off his/her performance or shifting the entire burden upon the people without showing way to them. In fact, facilitation means doing for doing. This broadly means, motivating, educating, organising, guiding, counselling, informing, suggesting, advising, helping, enabling, enhancing, equipping, training, orienting, tracking, capacity building etc. Hence NGO workers have to help the people help themselves and equip the people to do by themselves. Otherwise facilitation would mean evasion.
- NGOs have to explore more and more local funding than merely depending upon foreign sources. At the same time NGOs do not dilute their values for the sake of mobilising funds. Greasing the funding palms need to be avoided. This could be possible only through the joint action of good NGOs.

  NGOs have to explore the possibilities of raising local funds. Despite poverty, the country is blessed with many elites, opulent business magnates, industrialists, scientists, scholars, philanthropists etc., whose standard of living would equate or even excel the standards of westerners who contribute funds for this country. Hence NGOs can manifest their good works to such potential donars and imbue a sense in them of their social obligation to extend their benevolant hands to the suffering fellow-beings of this nation.
- NGOs must not close their eyes and ears when they come across corruptive and unethical practices and should not conform to the existing ill-systems (saying 'Yes' for everything) but to transform the same for the cause of the poor and betterment of the society as a whole. Just because everybody does, NGOs also need not do the same. Wrong is wrong even if everybody does it. NGOs need not be one among the Ninety Nine wrong doers but to be the One unique Right Thinker and Right Doer. Otherwise they cannot be called agents of social change.
- NGOs need not be confined to grass-root level community organisations only. Their wisdom shall rise up to the level of policy framers and law makers. For instance, Budgets are the indicators of

Government Policies. NGOs can read between the lines of states' and central budget, critically analyse the allocation to each sector and introspect how far poor rural communities are being benefited. They can offer suggestions for modifications/alterations through media, reputed political spokesmen, opponent political representatives etc. In this regard such NGOs require economic experts and social scientists.

- Rules are framed usually in favour of the rule - makers to rule others. NGOs need to sensitively look into this and influence rule - framers, policy - designers and law - makers to plan things unprejudiciously. In specific, NGOs must facilitate policy - makers to earmark additional budget on the principle of positive discrimination (ie) a favour shown to oppressed ones in terms of caste, class and gender. In this context, NGOs' outlook must be wide and wisdom, par excellence.
- NGOs need to be Mission driven and not be Donor driven.
- All NGOs must realise that people are truly their masters. Of course money and resources come in the name of the people whom they want to serve. Funds are received from the Donating people at one end to the helpless people on the other. In between it passes through NGOs and that's all. Hence NGOs need not deem themselves as owners of such resources. They are truly answerable to the donating people. More so, they are morally, ethically and professionally accountable to the people for whose welfare resources are mobilised.
- Instead of NGOs directly implementing the project it would be better if NGOs facilitate the local Sangams or People's Organisations to execute the same on their own. Necessary skills and capacities can be built upon the people by the NGOs.
- Empowering the people is NGOs' priority so that people themselves can deal with issues like poverty and injustice.
- NGO's interventions must be highly process oriented and not product oriented.
- People must be involved not only in planning and implementation processes as many NGOs do but also in the evaluation and impact-assessment.
- People require capacities and not subsidies or gifts or charities. The vacuum of capacitilessness can be filled in with capacity building only.
- It is good to have qualified hands as development workers than raw ones. But it is important to have persons of profound commitment and innate special qualities. Some social workers may seem to do

hardwork (running about here and there for making money) but they may not be loyal and honest in their dealings. Services of such so - called social workers in voluntary organisation is like that of circulation of blood without red cells.

- NGO workers need to be reasonably paid in accordance with their performance or atleast to take care of their minimum livelihood. Personal life (family life) and their professional career are inter related to one another.
- Too less a pay given by NGOs may not gratify even their basic needs. At this juncture the workers may develop a tendency to grab certain resources meant for the people. Observations and studies reveal that development workers feel that their life would have been better if they were the beneficiaries of the NGO rather than the staff of the organisation.
- Advocacying and Lobbying could be effectively done through collective efforts of NGOs. Networking NGOs is an important requirement in the voluntary sector. Previous experiences and observations reveal that NGOs individually do the best but collectively the least. Several attempts were made by some NGO leaders, but networks and federations seem to be neither successful nor sustainable (except few).
- NGOs networks and federations must become a platform for information sharing and capacity building. NGOs, if necessary, have to network the various networks under one umbrella, in each district, as a federation which can offer professional guidance to NGOs and also the Government authorities to plan and execute development schemes in a Just manner. Such NGOs', federation must have a very broad vision to ensure structural transformation and social change without any ulterior inferior motives.
- NGOs are supposed to be only catalysts who could operate objectively, empathetically and professionally. They need to be change-agents of the society without themselves being changed by other forces.
- NGOs can avoid duplication of intervention where two or more NGOs happen to operate. They can jointly plan and mutually complement one another.
- There are six lakhs villages in the country. If we include the hamlets/ hutments also the number would be around eighteen lakhs as a whole. Why should NGOs duplicate and meddle in one and the same village with the same programme? They must reach the unreached unmindful of their personal inconveniences.

- NGOs tend to boast themselves more of their strength (i.e.) their Community work/field work. They forget the significance of the management part (i.e.) administering men, money, material and other resources. Hence NGOs have to promote planning, monitoring and evaluating systems. Organisation running with the mere strength of fieldwork alone is like that of a man walking with one stronger leg while the other happens to be a club-foot.
- NGOs are supposed to be good model organisations for the society in terms of professional ethics, social code and human values. NGOs need to develop a professional conscience as they are addressing social issues.
- NGOs have to the maximum reduce their over head charges, say 10%. Upto 90% of budget of the project must directly reach the people.
- All types of NGOs are needed in a country like India i.e. from charity types to empowering ones (as it is seen in chapter - 4). Instead of railing at the other, every NGO can complement one another. For instance in a disastered area a Charity NGO can provide food and clothing; Rehabilitation NGO can recontruct their houses; Development NGO can carryout economic development programmes while the Empowering one can enable the people to exercise control over the resources. In this way, NGOs can play collective and complementary role to develop the community as a whole. If feasible the same NGO can play multiple roles as stated earlier.

  It is understood that there does not exist a co-ordination/linkage between administrative staff and field staff and also between one unit and the other. Whenever needed the office staff can also be taken to the field for an exposure so that they can realise for whom at all they render their services, sitting in the office premises. Each one of the organisation needs to be constantly appraised of the mission of the NGO and the purpose of his/her existence in the same organisation.
- Weekly review meetings, monthly review meetings, quarterly review meetings, biannual internal evaluation, annual external evaluation etc., would enable NGOs to make self assessment and appraisal of progress which would eventually improve the systems within the organisation. Review includes everyone - not only the field staff but also office staff at all levels.
- They need to realise that every penny comes to them out of the pains, sufferings and sacrifices of the donars (and the Tax Payers) abroad or within the country. Good NGO need not look at other principleless organisations who prosper suddenly through inferior means. People

are the best judges of the NGOs and only good NGOs will sustain in the field in the long run.

- NGOs should not substitute people's role. They can only facilitate them.
- NGO persons need to function as Development philosophers of social change and transformation. Trivial minded cannot perform triumphal social experiments.
- NGOs can collaborate with other actors of development be it Government, Bank, resource agencies, legal bodies and other organisations. They can extend only critical collaboration and not subdued or comfortable cooperation.
- Voluntary work must be an outcome of a preferred choice of any individual or members of the organisation and not a profit making chance. The latter would jeopardise voluntary sector.
- NGO have to play the role of sensitizing the other like minded NGOs also. If situation demands they also have to transform the other raw NGOs. Evil elements should be discouraged to simulate to be charitable and developmental.
- NGOs can avoid or at the maximum minimise double standards. NGOs must be principle centered organisations. The highest NGO principle is nothing but people centered intervention.
- Development work is no longer a favour to the poor. It is people's legitimate right and NGOs have to rightly understand it.
- NGOs can avoid raising funds from imperfect systems. Resources coming from imperfect systems cannot be useful to correct the imperfect Social practices.
- One of the highest skills required for NGOs is application of common sense despite the well designed objectives and well articulated strategies. Common sense application means 'prioritised interventions distinguishing between the most essential and least essential things'.
- Networking of people's organisations is the key and most significant function of today's NGOs. At the grass-root level CBOs (Community Based Organisations) need to be organised like SHGs, VDAs, Co-ops, Workers' societies and so on as required. These community based people's organisations need to be federated. These federations (promoted by different NGOs) need to be networked into people's institutions. Thus large and large numbers of people's federations / institutions of common objectives have to be strategically united and allied though there may be certain specific diversities. History reveals that 'increase in number of people and be united means

increase in power and solidarity. Division and fragmentation means loss of power and control and an ultimate fall'.

- So NGOs apart from their individual endeavour, have to collectively work together to form large alliances of various people's bodies so that they can gain a 'massive strength' to encounter the macro interventions monitered by macro power bases.
- In this regard, NGOs' collective work becomes paramountly crucial and inevitable.
- NGOs, by and large, work for the sustainability of the people but hardly think about their own sustainability. They need to work out plans for the sustainability of the programmes, finance and personnel of the organisations.

An NGO has four key internal functions i.e. (1) survival, (2) maintenance, (3) sustainability, (4) growth. This goes on like a cycle. If the sustainability function fails, the jouney of the organisation suddenly ends at a dead end or a blind corner. Growth follows the sustainability of the present state of affairs of the NGO.

NGOs need to learn a lot on the sphere of 'Management' in various aspects like personnel management, financial management, material management, marketting management, time management, keeping up punctuality, documentation, records keeping, scientific planning, process monitoring, co-ordination between office and field, collaboration between inter and intra sections the staff of disciplined administration, staff policy and their career development, office management, public relations etc. In fact, they must unlearn many things and learn managerial skills.

Dr. Y.C. James Yen, Founder of International Institute of Rural Reconstruction, Philippines gives the following development approach as the credo of rural construction movement.

Go to the poor people
Live among them
Learn from them
Plan with them
Work with them
Start with what they know
Build on what they have
Teach by showing, learn by doing
Not a showcase but a pattern
Not odds and ends but a system

Not piecemeal but integrated approach
Not to confirm but to transform
Not relief but release.

Conclusion

NGOs have done spectacular works in the field of rural development such as community health, agriculture, horticulture, social forestry, water shed development, animal husbandry, small scale industries, adult education, community organisation, sangam-formation, promotion of Self Help Groups, networking etc.

But still the work to be done is vast and wide as in the words of Robert Frost "miles to go before I sleep".

NGOs need to become more and more professional.

Their work must be unique like an Oasis in the desert that must be sensible, visible, useful, beneficial, superb, sustainable and replicable and not like a mirage.

The time has come that the NGOs have to render expertised services and to perform challenging roles. However mighty projects NGOs implement, whatever model projects they have carried out, poor masses in this large country will continue to remain poor only unless Policies and rules are made in favour of the poor and the oppressed. NGOs have to intellectually and strenuously work to make the policies pro-poor. Hence, in the current context of globalisation NGOs need to protect the poor and the marginalised from being exploited by the powerful elements.

The true success of NGO is not the receipt of national awards or getting international rewards but only the victory to the people over their poverty and injustices. I strongly believe that People's development is People's business and NGOs can facilitate them to accomplish their needs. Unfortunately NGOs are engrossed with their micro level activities. Every intervention must become a strategy and not just dead end in activity itself.

It does not matter whether it is a small NGO, or a big NGO or a large NGO or a mighty NGO or an old NGO or a young NGO, what matters is whether one is a Professional NGO with a profound commitment and persevering will. By professional NGO, I refer to "**the**" voluntary organisation to which people are its heart, commitment is its spinal card, professionalism is its brain and Integrity and honesty are its lungs. Strong in one aspect and weak in the other may not serve the purpose totally and completely. Hence a full fledged NGO must be committed, people centred, professional and honest.

I am hopeful that this book will serve as a tiny tool in actions and professionalising the performances of NGOs and I wish that NGOs of different styles will elevate their standards and work for the uplift of the rural poor. Reconstruction of the nation means 're-construction of the villages which necessitates untiring works, strategic facilitation 'and smart intervention of NGOs.

BIBLIOGRAPHY

Abraham, K. C., 'Marxism and Christianity in India' in *The Encounter of the Church with Movements of Social Change in Various Cultural Contexts*, Geneva, Lutheran World Federation, 1977.

Abrahamsson, B., *Bureaucracy or Participation*, Sage, 1977.

Alamgir, M.K., Participatory Development in Bangladesh : The Ulashi Jadunathpur Canal-Digging Project Geneva, ILO, 1978.

Alliband, T., *Catalysts of Development : Voluntary Agencies in India*, West Hartford, Kumarian Press, 1984.

Arole, R., A Comprehensive Rural Health Project in Jamkhed (India), *Contact*, 10, 1-11, 1982.

Asian NGO Coalition, The Case of Alternative Development, Niramit, Thailand, Asian NGO Coalition, 1979.

Association of Voluntary Agencies for Rural Development Two decades of avard : Report of activities 1958—79, New Delhi.

Ashford, Douglas E., *Ideology and Participation, Library of Social Research*, Vol. 3, Beverly Hills, Sage, 1972.

A Study of History, Roles and Future Challenges, Voluntary Development Organisations in India, Society for Participatory Research in Asia New Delhi, 1991.

Bajirao, B.U., 'Democratic Decentralisation and the Participation of the Underprivileged in the Development of Village Communities in India, Paper presented at the 10th World Congress of the International Sociological Association, 1982.

Bang, A., 'Economic Self-Sufficiency in Community Health Programme : Myth, Mirage and Nemesis', *Link*, 3, 3-6 1983.

Banking with the Poor. (SHG) Published NABARD, Hyderabad.

Batchelor, P., *People in Rural Development*, Exeter, Peternoster, 1981.

Baxi, U., 'For Bunker Roy, a Word of Advice', *Mainstream*, April 6, 8-31, 1985.

Baxi, U., Two Threats to Democratic Social Action, *Mainstream*,

XXIV(48) 25-32, 1986.

Bedi, Narinder, Development of Power in D. Rajasekhar (ed.) *Decentralised Government and NGOs : Issues, Strategies and Ways Forward Delhi*: Concept.

Benjamin, J., 'Voluntary Bodies and Rural Development', *Mainstream*, XXIV (46) 15-16, 1986.

Bhaduri, A. and Rahman, Md. A. (eds.) *Studies in Rural Participation*, New Delhi, Oxford Publishing House, 1982.

Bhat, M. K., Anita Cheria & edwin, Life goes on... sustainability of Community development programs and the withdrawal of NGO Support an enqiury into expectations and implications. The centre for innovation in Voluntary Action (CIVA), U.K., London, and Bangalore Consultance Office 1999.

Bhat, M. K., Sustainability and Local Governance. In. D. Rajasekhar (ed.), *Decentralised Government and NGOs : Issues, Strategies and Ways Forward*, Concept, 1999, Delhi.

Brill, E.J., *Volunteers*, Voluntary Associations and Development, International Institute of Sociology and Social Anthropology, 1981.

Bryant, C., Managing Rural Development : Peasant Participation in Rural Development, Development Monographs No. 1, (West Hartford, Kumarian Press, 1980.

Castillo, G.T., How Participatory is Participatory Development : A Review of the Philippines Experience (Manilla, Institute of Development Studies) 1983.

Centre for Agrarian Research, 1993. World Conference on Agrarian Reform & Rural Development. Role of NGOs, iii, p. 158, 1979.

Chambers, Robert, *Challenging the Professions : Frontiers for Rural Development*, New Delhi : Intermediate Technology Publications, 1993 kvi, 143p.

Chambers, R., *Rural Development : Putting the Last First*, Longman, 1983.

Charyulu, U.V.M., *Directory of NGOs in Rural Development India;* edited by U.V.N. Charyulu & V.K. Natarajan, Hyderabad, 1984, kii, 285 p. 309.

Charyulu, U.V.N., Voluntary Organisations and Rural Development : Case Study of Cudapah District Vyavasaya Ceela Sarvodaya Sangham / by U.V.N. Charyulu and V.K. Natarajan — Hyderabad : N.I.R.D., 1980 64p.

Chopra, Kanchan *et. al.*, *Participatory Development : People and Common Property Resources.* Sage Publications, New Delhi, 1990.

Christian Aid News, *Christian Aid* - London.

Combe, Simon, Indigenous Voluntary Agency Sector and Rural Change in India : Towards a destination - Department of Town and Country Planning, University of Sydney, Sydney, 1987.

Constantino – David, K. Issues in Community Organisation, *Community Development Journal,* 17, 3, 190-201, 1982.

Council for Advancement of People's Action and Rural Technology CAPART and Voluntary Organisations - Guidelines - New Delhi CAPART ii, 127p.

Danda, Ajit K., Studies on Rural Development experiences and issues Inter-India Publications, New Delhi-1984.

Dantawala, M.L., (ed.), *Social Change Through Voluntary Action* (ed.) by M. L. Dantawala, Harsh Sethi and Pravin Visaria, Sage, 1998, 199 p. New Delhi.

Deshpande, V.D., 'Code of Conduct for Rural Voluntary Agencies', *Economic and Political Weekly,* XXI (30), 1304-1306, 1986.

De Kadt, E., *Sociology and Development,* Tavistock Publications, 1974.

Economic Development Institute, Readings in Participation, Washington D.C., World Bank, 1986.

Edwards, Michael and David Hulme (eds.), *Non-governmental Organisations Performance and Accountability : Beyond the Magic Bullet,* London : Earthscan, 1995.

Edwards, Michael and David Hulme (1996). Too Close for Comfort? The Impact of Official Aid on Non-Governmental Organisations. *World Development,* 24 (b).

Edwin, Anita Cheria, An Earty to Inherit — Sustainable livelihood programs the rationale, experience and impact - The Association for Rural Poor, Chennai, January, 1999.

El Ghonemy, M.R., 'Rural Poverty : Can Participation Resolve it?' in *Food Agricultural Organisation, Studies on Agrarian Reform and Rural Poverty,* Rome, FAO, 1984.

Epstein, T.S., *South India : Yesterday, Today and Tomorrow,* Macmillan Press, 1973.

Farrington, John, Non-Governmental Organisations and the State in Asia ed. by John Farrington and others, New Delhi, Routledge, 1993. kkkii, 366 p.

Farrington, John, Sustainable Agriculture : *NGOs, GOs and the Rural Poor,* ed. by John Farrington and S. Satish - Hyderabad; Booklinks Corporation, 1995. k, 312 p.

Farrington, John *et. al,* (eds.), The Reluctant Partners? Non-Governmental Organisations, the State and Sustainable Agriculture London :

Routledge, 1993.

Fernandez, Aloyslus P., The MYRADA Experience : Working with the Government in Multilateral and Bilateral Projects, Bangalore MYRADA, 1996.

Fernandes, W. and Tandon, R., Participatory Research and Evaluation, New Delhi, Indian Social Institute, 1981.

Fernandes, W., *People's Participation in Development,* New Delhi, India Social Institute, 1981.

Fonseca, A.J., *Challenge of Poverty in India,* New Delhi, Indian Social Institute, 1971.

Fowler, Allen, Organisational Vision, Mission, and Strategic Planning, Paper presented during Development Management Course, at PRIYA, Delhi, 1997.

Franda, M., Voluntary Associations and Local Development in India : The Janata Phase, *Young India,* New Delhi, 1983.

Freire, P., *Conscientisation and Liberation,* Institute of Cultural Action, 1973.

Freire, P., *By Learning They Can Teach,* Dar Es Salam, University of Dar Es Salam, 1971.

Freire, P., *Pedagogy of the Oppressed,* Harmondsworth, Penguin, 1972.

Funglesang, A. and Chandler, D., Participation as a Process : What can we learn from Grameena Bank, Bangladesh, Norway, Ministry of Development Cooperation, 1986.

Gender Planning, Published by Centre for Health Education, Training and Nutrition Awareness Ahmedabad, Gujarat, 1994.

Giriappa, Issues in Rural Development, Daya Publishers, 1995. viii, 1554 p.

Griffith, Geoff, Poverty Alleviation for Rural Women : Indian Voluntary Organisations and Village Developments - Aldershot : Avebury, 1994, kv, 219 p.

Group Dynamics Experiment & Experience, Indian Bank, Madras 1992.

Gulhati, Kaval, *Strengthening Voluntary Action in India : Health-Planning, the Environment and Women's Development* by Ravi Gulhati and others, Konark Pubs. Delhi, 1995, kvi, 286 p.

Gultang, J., Peter O. and Roy, P., 'Self Reliance, A Strategy for Development' in F. Lisk (ed.), pp. 127-147, 1985.

Gupta, A., *Integrated Rural Development and Voluntary Agencies,* New Delhi, Indian Council for Social Science Research, 1978.

Hallove, Richard, NGO, Go Collaboration and Advocacy Paper presented during Development Management Course, at PRIYA, Delhi, 1997.

Harichandran, C., 'Futuristic Role of Voluntary Organisations', *Khadi Gramodyog,* 28 (7) 346-350, 1982.

Hazral Ali, U., *Involvement of Rural Poor in Development Through Local Organisation,* Commilla, Bangladesh Academy for Rural Development, 1980.

Holding together Collaborations and Partnerships in the Real World, Priya, New Delhi, 1995.

Holy Bible (New Testament) Pub. by India Bible Society, Bangalore, 1992.

Huque, W., *et. al.,* Towards a Theory of 'Rural Development', *Development Dialogue,* 2, 7-137, 1977.

Indian Institute of Rural Management, Introduction to Project Management, Kalyan Path, Police Memorial, Jaipu, 1993.

Indonesian Human Resources Development Foundation, Seminar on People's Participation in National Development, Denspasar, Seminar Reports, 1973.

Jain, L. C., *Grass Without Roots : Rural Development with Government Auspices,* New Delhi, Sage, 1985.

Jain, L.C., Debates in Voluntary Sector : Some Reflections in Voluntary Action and Government Control, A Paper.

Joel A.G.R. Bose, Role of Voluntary Organisations in Rural Development Thsesis submitted at Bharathidasan University, Tiruchirapalli, 1994.

Joel A.G.R. Bose, Case Study of Mahila Mandali in Chinayadara CASA IN ACTION, Chennai, Vol. 6 Issue 3 Sept., 1997.

Joel A.G.R. Bose, Cultivation on Lease Land a SHG Pogramme by Dalit Women, CASA IN ACTION, Chennai, Vol. 8, Issue 1 March, 199.

Joel A.G.R. Bose, A Collective initiative of Rural Women (MACS) CASA IN ACTION, Chennai Vol. 8, Issue 3, September, 1999.

Joel A.G.R. Bose,CASA's Experience with Self Help Groups, Participation and Governance Published by PRIA, New Delhi, July, 1997.

Joel A.G.R. Bose, Emerging role of NGOs paper presented in Avinasilingam College in Coimbatore, 1994.

Joel A.G.R. Bose, Role of NGOs paper presented in NGO conference at Hotel Ajantha, Trichy, 1996.

Joel A.G.R. Bose, Leadership and holistic development paper prsented in A.P. NGOs Conference at Vijayawada, 2000.

Joshi, S., *et al.* (eds.), Experience of Advocacy in Environment and Development, Bangalore DSI and NOVIB, 1997.

Kapoor, A. K., *Rural Development Through NGOs* by A. K. Kapoor and Dharamvir Singh, Rawat, Jaipur, 1997, p. 230.

Karat, P., 'Action Groups/Voluntary Organisations : A Factor in Imperialist

Strategy', *The Marxist,* 2 (2), 19-54, 1984.

Khanna, B.S, Participation of Non-Government Organisations (NGOs) in Integrated Rural Development : An overview — Comilla : CIRDAP study series No. 57, 309-263.

Kolawole, A., 'The Role of Grassroots Participation in National Development : Lessons from the Kwara State of Nigeria', *Community Development Journal,* 17, 2, 121-133, 1982.

Korten, D. C. and Klass, R., *People Centered Development : Contributions Toward Theory and Planning Frameworks,* West Hartford, Kumarian, Press, 1984.

Korten, David C, *Getting to the 21st Century; Voluntary Action and the Global Agenda* - Connecticut : Kumarian Press, p. 253, 1990.

Koshy, Key Note address CASA, Golden Jubilee Celebration, 1997.

Kothal, Krishna, Economic Impact of Rural Development Projects on Small Farmers. *Journal of Rural Development,* 13 (2), 1994.

Kramer, R.M., *Voluntary Organisations in the Welfare State,* Berkeley, California University Press, 1981.

Krishnamurthy, V., 'Voluntary Action in Rural Development : A Survey', *Kurukshetra,* XXXIV (1), 33-36, 1985.

Krishnamurthy, V., 'Voluntary Agencies and Rural Development', *Kurukshetra,* 30 (18), 4-7, 1982.

Kumar, R. Gopa, Foreign Contributions to Voluntary Organisations in India : A Geographical Analysis. INU, New Delhi (mimeo), 1999.

Lalitha, N.V., *Voluntary Work in India,* National Institute of Public Cooperation and Child Development, New Delhi, 1975.

Lele, U., *The Design of Rural Development,* Baltimore, John Hopkins University Press, 1975.

Lisser, J., *The Politics of Altruism,* Geneva, Lutheran World Federation, 1977.

Lutheran World Federation, The Identity of the Church and its Service to the Whole Human Being, Geneva, LWF.

Maheshwari, Shriram, *Rural Development in India : A Public Policy Approach,* 2nd ed., New Delhi : Sage Publications, 1995, 274 p.

Marsden, D. and Oakley, P., 'Radical Community Development in the Third World' in G. Craig *et. al.* (eds.), 1982, pp. 153-63.

Menon, A. Gopal Organisation and Administration of Voluntary Action in Andhra Pradesh : Basic Data of Voluntary Agencies for Rural Development in Andhra Pradesh - Hyderabad : Central University of Hyderabad 1992, 88 p.

Midgley, J. *et. al., Community Participation, Social Development and the State,* Methuen, 1986.

Mishra, Madhu, Directory of Voluntary and Other Organisations in Rural Development, Calcutta : Indian Institute of Management, 1992..

Misra, Sunil (ed.), *Voluntary Action in Health and Population : Dynamics of Social Transition,* Sage, p. 273, New Delhi, 2000.

Mohanty, Manoranjan, ed., Foreign Aid and NGO's — New Delhi : Voluntary Action Network India, 1996, p. 341.

Mohanty, Priyabrata, 1991, Role of NGOs in Rural Development with Special Reference to Self-Employment; conducted in Nuagan Block, Puri Dist. Orissa, Hyderabad, NIRD, 1993, 61p. Dissertation.

Mukerjee, P. N., 'Social Movements and Social Change : Towards a Conceptual Clarification and Theoretical Framework', *Sociological Bulletin,* 26 (1), 1977.

Murthy, R.K. and Nitya Rao, Indian NGOs, Poverty Alleviation and their Capacity Enhancement in the 1990s : An Institutional and Social Relations Perspective, New Delhi : FFS, 1997.

Nagaraja & M. K. Bhat, Building Civil Society, India Civil Society Collective, Bangalore, 2000.

Napoleon Hill, Success through a Positive Mental Attitude.

National Institute of Public Cooperation and Child Development, Report of the Seminar on Role of Voluntary Agencies in Rural Development, New Delhi - August 25-27, 1981, New Delhi.

National Institute of Rural Development, Voluntary Development Organisations in India : A Study of History. *Roles and Future Challenges,* New Delhi : PRIA, 1991.

National Institute of Rural Development, National Workshop of Rule of Voluntary Organisations in Rural Development; with special reference to women July 5-6, 1982 - background material — Hyderabad, 1982 vp. (Mimeo).

National Institue of Rural Development, Course on Management of Voluntary Organisations of Rural Development November, 21-30, 1985 : Reading Material - Hyderabad, 1985, viii, 182 p. (Mimeo)

Namerta Income and Employment Generation Programmes of NGOs in India. Bangalore : Development Support Initiative, 1999.

National Institute of Rural Development Course on Voluntary Organisations and Rural Development, 7th - 13th January, 1982 - Reading Material — Hyderabad, p. 247+27, 1982. (Mimeo).

National Institute of Rural Development, Course on Management of Voluntary Organisations of Rural Development, November, 21-30, 1985; Reading Material — Hyderabad, p. 182, 1985.

Oakley, P., 'Continuing Inquiry into Participation in Development in the Third World', *Community Development Journal*, 17, 3, 259-262, 1982.

O'Hearn, Shawna Anna, Prerequisites which foster change in Rural Community Development - A Case Study of Drinking Water Initiatives in Gujarat - Ann Arbor, UMI, p. 155, 1996.

Oommen, T. K., *Social Transformation in Rural India,* New Delhi, Vikas, 1984.

Oommen, T.K., *Charisma, Stability and Change : An Analysis of Bhoodan-Gramdan Movement in India,* Thomson Press, New Delhi, 1972b.

Overseas Development Institute, Proceedings of the Conference on NGOs in Development, ODA, 1987.

Padron, M., NGOs and Grass Roots Development : Limits and Possibilities, The Hague, Institute of Social Studies, 1982.

Pamela Dix, Philip Holden Super Success, Discover your true potential and get what you want out of life; 1996.

Pant, Niranjan, Role of the Government Bureaucracy and the Non-Governmental Organisation in the Rural Development of India; A Case Study in District in Northern India by Niranjan Pant and Others, Tokyo : Institute of Developing Economics, p. 193. (Joint Research Programme Series No. 105).

Participatory Study of the Poor Household Economy of Gujarat, towrds understanding the impact of structural adjustment programme (SAP) UNNATI, 1997.

Partners in Progress, Experiences of Voluntary Organizations in India, St. Paul's Publications, Bangalore, 1997.

Patel, A.R., Rural Development : A Challenging Task for Voluntary Agencies, *Kurukshetra,* XXXIV (1), 24-28, 1985.

Paul Hersey, Kenneth H. Blanchard, Management of Organizational Behaviour Utilizing Human Resources, Prentice Hall of India Private Ltd., New Delhi, 1988.

People's Action for Development Conference of Coordinating Agencies with networks in the voluntary section in rural development 19-20 April 1985 — New Delhi : PAD, 1985, p. 64.

People's Action for Development India, Report of National Convention on Collaboration among NGOs, unpublished, 1885.

Planning Commission, Report on NGOs, New Delhi, Government of India, Undated.

Prasad, Anirudh, Voluntary Action and Rural Reconstruction : The Gram Bharti, 1998.

Rahema, M., 'The Growing Role of NGOs : Autonomous Actors or Part of the Delivery System?' Society for International Development, 18th World Conference Paper C.1.6, Rome, 1985.

Rajasekhar, D. and N. L. Narasimha Reddy, Local Development Programmes and NGOs : A Guide on Local Government Programmes for Field Workers. Bangalore : DSI, 1997.

Rajasekhar, D., Decemtralised Government and NGOs, Issues, Strategies and Ways Forward, Ashok Kumar Mittal, Concept Publishing Company, New Delhi, 1999.

Rajasekhar, D., Impact of Micro-Finance Programmes on Poverty and Gender Equality; Evidence from Indian NGOs'. UNIRSD Discussion Paper, (Forthcoming), Geneva, 2000.

Rajasekhar, D., Problems and Prospects of Group lending in NGO Credit Programmes in Inida. *Savings and Development*, 20 (1), 1996.

Rajasekhar, D., Rural Development Strategies of NGOs. *Journal of Social and Economic Development*, 1 (2), 1998.

Rajasekhar, Working paper 66, Non-governmental Organisations in India: Opportunities and Challenges, Institute for Social and Economic Change, 2000.

Ramamurthy, S.R., 'Government Functionaries Must Wholeheartedly Accept Voluntary 'Agencies', *Kurukshetra*, XXXIV (1), 10-13, 1985.

Reddy, N.L. Narasimha and D. Rajasekhar, Development Programmes and NGOs : A Guide on Central Government Programmes for NGOs in India. Bangalore : BCO and NOVIB, 1996.

Regional Seminar on Involvement of Youth and Voluntary Organisations in Rural Development (August 6-8, 1986) - Hyderabad, 1986. v.p. (Mimeo).

Report on Workshop on Panchayat Raj Institution Consequent to 73rd and 74th Constitutional Amendment Acts Workshop Report - CASA - New Delhi.

Riddel, R. and Mark Robinson, The Impact of NGO Poverty Alleviation Projects : Results of the Case Study Evaluations.' Working Paper No. 68, London : Overseas Development Institute, 1992.

Rigby, A., Practical Utopianism : A Gandhian Approach to Rural Community Development in India', *Community Development Journal*, 20, 1, 2-9 (1995).

Robinson, M., Governance, Democracy and Conditionality : NGOs and the New Policy Agenda. In A. Clayton (ed.) *Governance, Democracy and Conditionality : What Role for NGOs?* Oxford : INTRAC, 1993.

Roy, R., *Bureaucracy and Development*, New Delhi, Manas, 1975.

Roy, Sanjit, 'NGOs — Changing Role', *Seminar*, 273, 30-33, 1982.

Roy, Sanjit, 'Let Voluntary Agencies Plan Their Own Schemes, *Kurukshetra*, XXXIV (1) 8-9 and 13, 1985b.

Rustom S. Davar, General Management, Progressive Corporation Pvt. Ltd., Bombay, 1966.

Ruttan, V.W., 'Integrated Rural Development Programmes : A Historical Perspective', *World Development*, 12, 4, 398, 1984.

Sangitha, S.N. 'Self-employment Programme for Rural Youth. The Role of Non-governmental Organisation (NGOs) *IIMB Management Review*, 5 (2), 1990.

Seminar on Agrarian Reforms and Rural Development Role of NGOs, the Report Part-I, 9-11 January, 1979, Promoted by FAO FFHC/AD — Bangkok : Centre for Agrarian Research, Training & Education (CARTE), Ghaziabad, vi, p. 32, 1979.

Sen, Jai, On Anti-Voluntarism. *Lokayan Bulletin*, 4 (3/4), 9-37, 1986.

Sen, Siddhartha, Some Aspects of State-NGO Relationships in India in the Post-Independence Era. *Development and Change*, Vol. 30. 327-355, 1999.

Sethi, Harsh, 'Rural Development : Alternate Strategies', *Economic and Political Weekly*, Special Number, 1978.

SEWA BANK, Booklets Published by SEWA, Ahmedabad, 1997.

Sharan, S. V., Role of Civil Society in facilitating empowerment of the poor and the marginalised.

Sharma, Manoj, Health Promotion through Community Action : Health Orientation Training for Development Workers, a manual by Manoj Sharma and Shiv Kumar Singh - New Delhi : Voluntary Health Association of India, 96 p., 1991.

Shetty, Salil, Occasional paper Series No. 3, Development Project in Assessing Empowerment, Society for Participatory Research in India, New delhi, 1997.

Singh, Anil K., Non-governmental Organisations : Guidelines for Good Policy and Practice, Voluntary Action Network, India, Vani, New Delhi.

Singhal, C.S., Voluntary Action in Rural Development : A Study of Volunteers in Assam, New Delhi : Omsons Publications, p. 119, 1998.

Sommer, J.G. *et. al.*, Rural Development at the Grassroots — The Catalysts Role, New Delhi, Ford Foundation, 1974.

Srivastava, U.K., Planning and Implementation of Rural Development Projects by a Voluntary Agency : A Study of Bhartiya Agro-Industries Foundation, Uruli Kanchan, Poona, by U.K. Srivastava and others - Ahmedabad : I.I.M., ik, p. 289.

Srivastava, Uma Kant, Rural Development in Action : The Experience of a Voluntary agency / by Uma Kant Srivastava and P.S. George — Bombay, Somaiya, 1977, ik, 205 p.

Stephen, F., NGOs : Hope of the Last Decade of this Century. Bangalore: *SEARCH*, 1990.

Strengthening the Grass-Roots, Nature and Role of Support Organizations. PRIA, New Delhi, 1995.

Structural Adjustment Programmes : An Annotated Bibliography, New Delhi : Voluntary Action Network India, 1997.

Study Materials on People Centered Development, Womens Empowernnent, Strategic planning Operational Management and NGO, GO Collaboration as a part of Development Management Course by PRIA, New Delhi, between January and April, 1997.

Summaries of Studies of Faculty of Human Resource Development (1986-1993) - Hyderabad, NIRD, 1993.

Sundaram I. S. (1986) Voluntary Agencies and Rural Development, New Delhi BR Publishing Corporation.

Tandon, Rajesh and Anuj Jain, Management of Voluntary Organisations, Society for Participatory Research in Asia, New delhi, 1993.

Thandon, Rajesh, People Centered Development Paper presented during Development Management Course, at PRIYA, Delhi, 1997.

Thiruvelluvar, Thirukkural, Pub. by Manimegalai Press, Madras, 1995.

Vettivel, Surendra K., Community Participation Theory and Practice Vetri Publishers, New Delhi, 1995.

Vohra, Gautam, Altering Structures : Innovative Experiments at the Grassroots - Bombay : Tata Institute of Social Sciences, p. 225, 1990.

Voluntary Development Organisations in India : A Study of History, Roles and Future Challenges, PRIA, New Delhi, 1991.

Voswanath, Vanita, *NGOs and Women's Development in Rural South India: A Comparative Analysis*, Vistaar Publications, New Delhi, 1993, kv, 179 p.

Walls, A.F., Evangelical Views and Development, *Christian Aid.*

Webster, Neil, The Role of NGO's in Indian Rural Development : Some Lessons from West Bengal and Karnataka, *The European Journal of Development Research*, 7 (2), 1992.

Weisgru, Makine Kay, Social and Political Relations of Development : NGOs and Adivasi Bhils in Rural Rajasthan, Ann Arbor : UMI, p. 315, 1993.

Workshop on Project Formulation and Implementation in Voluntary Sector (June 19-25, 1995) Hyderabad; N.I.R.D., p. 112, 1995.

Yojana, Special Issue on Voluntary Agencies, 28, 20 and 21 November, 1984.

Youth and Voluntarism, New Delhi : Voluntary Action Network India, New Delhi, 1995.

INDEX